Bergson And His Philosophy

by

John Alexander Gunn

ABOUT THE AUTHOR

John Alexander Gunn (1896–1975) was a distinguished philosopher whose academic journey took him from the University of Liverpool to the University of Melbourne. He earned his Ph.D. from the University of Liverpool, where he honed his philosophical acumen. In 1923, Gunn's scholarly pursuits led him to the University of Melbourne, where he assumed the esteemed role of a professor. His tenure at the university spanned several years until his retirement in 1938. Following his retirement, Colin R. Badger succeeded him as the Director of Extension, carrying forward the legacy of academic leadership. Throughout his illustrious career, John Alexander Gunn penned several notable books, each contributing to the realm of philosophy. Among his literary achievements, "Bergson and His Philosophy" (1920) stands as a masterpiece, showcasing his deep understanding of the philosopher Henri Bergson and his profound ideas. Gunn's intellectual curiosity extended to various facets of philosophy, evident in his works such as "Modern French Philosophy: a Study of the Development Since Comte" (1922), "Wealth" (1924), "Benedict Spinoza" (1925), "Livelihood" (1927), "The Problem of Time: An Historical & Critical Study" (1929), and "Spinoza, The Maker Of Lenses" (1932). These works delve into diverse philosophical subjects, reflecting Gunn's versatility and scholarly rigor.

CONTENTS

PREFACE

The aim of this little work is practical, and it is put forth in the hope that it may be useful to the general reader and to the student of philosophy as an introduction and guide to the study of Bergson's thought. The war has led many to an interest in philosophy and to a study of its problems. Few modern thinkers will be found more fascinating, more suggestive and stimulating than Bergson, and it is hoped that perusal of the following pages will lead to a study of the writings of the philosopher himself. This is a work whose primary aim is the clear exposition of Bergson's ideas, and the arrangement of chapters has been worked out strictly with that end in view. An account of his life is prefixed. An up-to-date bibliography is given, mainly to meet the needs of English readers; all the works of Bergson which have appeared in England or America are given, and the comprehensive list of articles is confined to English and American publications. The concluding chapters endeavour to estimate the value of Bergson's thought in relation to Politics (especially Syndicalism), Ethics, Religion, and the development of thought generally.

My thanks are due to Professor Mair, Professor of Philosophy in the University of Liverpool, for having read the MS. while in course of preparation, for contributing an introduction, for giving some helpful criticism and suggestions, and, what is more, for stimulus and encouragement given over several years of student life.

Professor Bergson has himself expressed his approval of the general form of treatment, and I am indebted to him for information on a number of points. To Dr. Gillespie, Professor of Philosophy at Leeds, I am indebted for a discussion of most of the MS. following the reading of it. My thanks are also due to Miss Margaret Linn, whose energetic and careful assistance in preparing the MS. for the press was invaluable. I wish also to acknowledge kindness shown in supplying information on certain points in connexion with the bibliography by Mr. F. C. Nicholson, Librarian of the University of Edinburgh, by Mr. R. Rye, Librarian to the University of London, and by the University of London Press. I am grateful to Professor Bergson and to the Delegates of the Oxford University Press for permission to quote from La Perception du Changement, the lectures given at Oxford. Further I must acknowledge permission accorded to me by the English publishers of Bergson's works to quote passages directly from these authorized translations — To Messrs. Geo. Allen & Unwin, Ltd. (Time and Free Will and Matter and Memory), to Messrs. Macmillan & Co., Ltd. (Creative Evolution, Laughter, Introduction to Metaphysics), and to T. Fisher Unwin, Ltd. (Dreams). Through the kindness of M. Louis Michaud, the Paris publisher, I have been enabled to reproduce (from his volume of selections, Henri Bergson: Choix de textes et etude de systeme philosophique, Gillouin) a photograph of Bergson hitherto unpublished in this country.

J.A.G.

THE UNIVERSITY, LIVERPOOL March, 1920

INTRODUCTION

The stir caused in the civilized world by the writings of Bergson, particularly during the past decade, is evidenced by the volume of the stream of exposition and comment which has flowed and is still flowing. If the French were to be tempted to set up, after the German manner, a Bergson-Archiv they would be in no embarrassment for material, as the Appendix to this book—limited though it wisely is—will show. Mr. Gunn, undaunted by all this, makes a further, useful contribution in his unassuming but workmanlike and well-documented account of the ideas of the distinguished French thinker. It is designed to serve as an introduction to Bergson's philosophy for those who are making their first approach to it, and as such it can be commended.

The eager interest which has been manifested in the writings of M. Bergson is one more indication, added to the many which history provides, of the inextinguishable vitality of Philosophy. When the man with some important thought which bears upon its problems is forthcoming, the world is ready, indeed is anxious, to listen. Perhaps there is no period in recorded time in which the thinker, with something relevant to say on the fundamental questions, has had so large and so prepared an audience as in our own day. The zest and expectancy with which men welcome and listen to him is almost touching; it has its dangerous as well as its admirable aspects. The fine enthusiasm for the physical and biological sciences, which is so noble an attribute of the modern mind, has far from exhausted itself, but the almost boundless hope which for a time accompanied it has notably abated. The study of the immediate problems centring round the concepts of matter, life, and energy goes on with undiminished, nay, with intensified, zeal, but in a more judicious perspective. It begins to be noticed that, far from leading us to solutions which will bring us to the core of reality and furnish us with a synthesis which can be taken as the key to experience, it is carrying the scientific enquirer into places in which he feels the pressing need of Philosophy rather than the old confidence that he is on the verge of abolishing it as a superfluity. The former hearty and self-assured empiricism of science is giving way before the outcome of its own logic and a new and more promising spirit of reflection on its own "categories" is abroad. Things are turning out to be very far from what they seemed. The physicists have come to a point where, it may be to their astonishment, they often find themselves talking in a way which is suspiciously like that of the subjective idealist. They have made the useful discovery that if you sink your shaft deep enough in your search for reality you come upon Mind. Here they are in a somewhat unfamiliar region, in which they may possibly find that other instruments and other methods than those to which they have been accustomed are required. At any rate, they and the large public which hangs upon their words show a growing inclination to be respectful to the philosopher and an anxiety (sometimes an uncritical anxiety) to hear what he has to say.

No one needs to be reminded of the ferment which is moving in the world of social affairs, of the obscure but powerful tendencies which are forcing society out of its grooves and leaving it, aspiring but dubious, in new and uncharted regions. This may affect different minds in different ways. Some regret it, others rejoice in it; but all are aware of it. Time-honoured political and economic formulae are become "old clothes" for an awakened and ardent generation, and before the new garments are quite ready; the blessed word "reconstruction" is often mentioned. Men are not satisfied that society has really developed so successfully as it might have done; many believe that it finds itself in a cul-de-sac. But what is to be done? The experienced can see that many of the offered reforms are but the repetition of old mistakes which will involve us in the unhappy cycle of disillusion and failure. It is not to be wondered at, therefore, if men everywhere are seeking for a sign, a glimpse of a scheme of life, a view of reality, a hint of human destiny and the true outcome of human effort, to be an inspiration and a guide to them in their pathetic struggle out of the morass in which they, too obviously, are plunged. If Philosophy has anything to say which is to the point, then let Philosophy by all means say it. They are ready to attend. They may indeed expect too much from it, as those who best grasp the measure of Philosophy's task would be the first to urge.

This is the opportunity of the charlatan. Puzzled and half-desperate, we strongly feel the influence of the need to believe, are prone to listen to any gospel. The greater its air of finality and assurance the stronger is its appeal. But it is the opportunity also of the serious and competent thinker, and it is fortunate for the world that one of M. Bergson's quality is forthcoming. He is too wise a man, he knows the history of human thought too well, he realizes too clearly the extent of the problem to pretend that his is the last word or that he has in his pocket the final solution of the puzzle of the universe and the one and only panacea for human distresses. But he has one of the most subtle and penetrating intellects acting in and upon the world at this moment, and is more worthy of attention than all the charlatans. That he has obtained for himself so great an audience is one of the most striking and hopeful signs of the present time.

It is the more impressive inasmuch as Bergson cannot be said to be an easy author. The originality and sweep of his conceptions, the fine and delicate psychological analysis in which he is so adept and which is necessary for the development of his ideas—e.g., in his exposition of duree—make exacting demands upon those readers who wish to closely follow his thought. An interesting fact is that this is realized most of all by those who come to Bergson with a long process of philosophical discipline behind them. It is not surprising when we remember what he is trying to do, namely, to induce philosophical thought to run in new channels. The general reader has here an advantage over the other, inasmuch as he has less to unlearn. In the old words, unless we become as little children we cannot enter into this kingdom; though it is true that we do not remain as little children once entry is made. This is a serious difficulty for the hard-bitten philosopher who at considerable pains has formed conceptions, acquired a technique, and taken an orientation towards life and the universe which he cannot dismiss in a moment. It says much for the charitable spirit of Bergson's fellow-philosophers that they have given so friendly and hospitable a reception to his disturbing ideas, and so essentially humane a man as he must have been touched by this. The Bahnbrecher has his troubles, no doubt, but so also have those upon whose minds he is endeavouring to operate. Reinhold, one of Kant's earliest disciples, ruefully stated, according to Schopenhauer's story, that it was only after having gone through the Critique of Pure Reason five times with the closest and most scrupulous attention that he was able to get a grasp of Kant's real meaning. Now, after the lapse of a century and a half, Kant to many is child's play compared with Bergson, who differs more fundamentally from Kant than the Scoto-German thinker did from Leibniz and Hume. But this need not alarm the general reader who, innocent of any very articulate philosophical preconceptions, may indeed find in the very "novelty" of Bergson's teaching a powerful attraction, inasmuch as it gives effective expression to thoughts and tendencies moving dimly and half-formed in the consciousness of our own epoch, felt rather than thought. In this sense Bergson may be said to have produced a "philosophy for the times." In one respect Bergson has a marked advantage over Kant, and indeed over most other philosophers, namely, in his recognized masterly control over the instrument of language. There is a minimum of jargon, nothing turgid or crabbed. He reminds us most, in the skill and charm of his expression, of Plato and Berkeley among the philosophers. He does not work with so fine and biting a point as his distinguished countryman and fellow-philosopher, Anatole France, but he has, nevertheless, a burin at command of remarkable quality. He is a master of the succinct and memorable phrase in which an idea is etched out for us in a few strokes. Already, in his lifetime, a number of terms stamped with the impress of Bergson's thought have passed into international currency. In this connexion, has it been remarked that while an Englishman gave to the French the term "struggle for life," a Frenchman has given to us the term elan vital? It is worthy of passing notice and gives rise to reflections on the respective national temperaments, fanciful perhaps, but interesting. It is not, however, under the figure of the etcher's art or of the process of the mint that we can fully represent Bergson's resources of style. These suggest staccato effects, hard outlines, and that does not at all represent the prose of this writer. It is a fine, delicately interwoven, tissue-like fabric, pliant and supple. If one were in the secret of M. Bergson's private thoughts, it might be discovered that he does not admire his style so much as others do, for his whole manner of thought must, one suspects, have led him often to attempt to express the inexpressible. The ocean of life, that fluide bienfaisant in which we are immersed, has no doubt often proved too fluid even for him. "Only the understanding has a language," he almost ruefully declares in L'Evolution creatrice; and the understanding is, for him, compared with intuition peu de chose. Yet we can say that in what he has achieved his success is remarkable. The web of language which he weaves seems to fit and follow the movements of his thought as the skin ripples over the moving muscles of the thoroughbred. And this is not an accidental or trivial fact. M. Bergson may possibly agree with Seneca that "too much attention to style does not become a philosopher," but the quality of his thought and temperament does not allow him to express himself otherwise than lucidly. Take this, almost at random, as a characteristic example. It must be given, of course, in the original:

"L'intelligence humaine, telle que nous la representons, n'est point du tout celle que nous montrait Platon dans l'allegorie de la caverne. Elle n'a pas plus pour fonction de regarder passer des ombres vaines que de contempler, en se retournant derriere elle, l'astre eblouissant. Elle a autre chose a faire. Atteles comme des boeufs de labour, a une lourde tache, nous sentons le jeu de nos muscles et de nos articulations, le poids de la charrue et la resistance du sol: agir et se savoir agir, entrer en contact avec la realite et meme la vivre, mais dans la measure seulement ou elle interesse l'oeuvre qui s'accomplit et le sillon qui se creuse, voila la fonction de l'intelligence humaine."

That is sufficiently clear; we may legitimately doubt whether it is an adequate account of the function of the human intelligence, but we cannot be in any doubt as to what the view is; and more than that, once we have become acquainted with it, we are not likely to forget it.

For the student as yet unpractised in philosophical reflection, Bergson's skill and clarity of statement, his fertility in illustration, his frequent and picturesque use of analogy may be a pitfall. It all sounds so convincing and right, as Bergson puts it, that the critical faculty is put to sleep. There is peril in this, particularly here, where we have to deal with so bold and even revolutionary a doctrine. If we are able to retain our independence of judgment we are bound sooner or later, in spite of Bergson's persuasiveness, to have our misgivings. After all, we may begin to reflect, he has been too successful, he has proved too much. In attempting to use, as he was bound to do, the intelligence to discredit the intelligence he has been attempting the impossible. He has only succeeded in demonstrating the authority, the magisterial power, of the intelligence. No step in Philosophy can be taken without it. What are Life, Consciousness, Evolution, even Movement, as these terms are employed by Bergson, but the symbolization of concepts which on his own showing are the peculiar products of the human understanding or intelligence? It seems, indeed, on reflection, the oddest thing that Philosophy should be employed in the service of an anti-intellectual, or as it would be truer to call it a supra-intellectual, attitude. Philosophy is a thinking view of things. It represents the most persistent effort of the human intelligence to satisfy its own needs, to attempt to solve the problems which it has created: in the familiar phrase, to heal the wounds which it has itself made. The intellect, therefore, telling itself that it is incompetent for this purpose, is a strange, and not truly impressive, spectacle.

We are not enabled to recover from the sense of impotency thus created by being referred to "intuition." Bergson is not the first to try this way out. It would be misleading, no doubt, to identify him with the members of the Scottish School of a hundred years ago or with Jacobi; he reaches his conclusion in another way, and that conclusion is differently framed; nevertheless, in essence there is a similarity, and Hegel's comments [Footnote: Smaller Logic, Wallace's translation, c. v.] on Bergson's forerunners will often be found to have point with reference to Bergson himself.

It is hardly conceivable that any careful observer of human experience would deny the presence and power of intuition in that experience. The fact is too patent. Many who would not give the place to intuition which is assigned to it by Bergson would be ready to say that there may be more in the thrilling and passionate intuitive moments than Philosophy, after an age-long and painful effort, has been able to express. All knowledge, indeed, may be said to be rooted in intuition. Many a thinker has been supported and inspired through weary years of inquiry and reflection by a mother-idea which has come to him, if not unsought yet uncompelled, in a flash of insight. But that is the beginning, not the end, of his task. It is but the raw material of knowledge, knowledge in potentia. To invert the order is to destroy Philosophy not to serve it, is, indeed, a mere counsel of desperation. An intuitive Philosophy so-called finds itself sooner or later, generally sooner, in a blind alley. Practically, it gives rise to all kinds of crude and wasteful effort. It is not an accident that Georges Sorel in his Reflexions sur la Violence takes his "philosophy" from Bergson or, at least, leans on him. There are intuitions and intuitions, as every wise man knows, as William James once ruefully admitted after his adventures with nitrous oxide, or as the eaters of hashish will confess. To follow all our intuitions would lead us into the wildest dervish dance of thought and action and leave us spent and disheartened at the end. "Agnosticism" would be too mild a term for the result. Our intuitions have to be tried and tested; there is a thorny and difficult path of criticism to be traversed before we can philosophically endorse them and find peace of mind. What Hoffding says is in a sense quite true: "When we pass into intuition we pass into a state without problems." But that is, as Hoffding intends us to understand, not because all problems are thereby solved, but because they have not yet emerged. If we consent to remain at that point, we refuse to make the acquaintance of Philosophy; if we recognize the problems that are really latent there, we soon realize that the business of Philosophy is yet to be transacted.

The fact is that in this part of his doctrine—and it is an important part—the brilliant French writer, in his endeavours to make philosophizing more concrete and practical, makes it too abstract. Intuition is not a process over against and quite distinct from conceptual thought. Both are moments in the total process of man's attempt to come to terms with the universe, and too great emphasis on either distorts and falsifies the situation in which we find ourselves on this planet. The insistence on intuition is doubtless due, at bottom, to Bergson's admiration for the activity in the creative artist. The border-line between Art and Philosophy becomes almost an imaginary line with him. In the one case as in the other we have, according to him, to get inside the object by a sort of sympathy. True, there is this difference, he says, that aesthetic intuition achieves only the individual—which is doubtful—whereas the philosophic intuition is to be conceived as a "recherche orientee dans la meme sens que l'art, indeed, but qui prendrait pour objet la vie en general." He fails to note, it may be observed, that the expression of the aesthetic intuition, that is to say, Art, is always fixed and static. This in view of other aspects of his doctrine is remarkable. But apart from this attempt to practically identify Art and Philosophy—a hopeless attempt—there is, of course, available as a means of explanation the well-known and not entirely deplorable tendency of the protestant and innovator to overstate his case, to bring out by strong emphasis the aspect with which he is chiefly concerned and which he thinks has been unduly neglected. This, as hinted, has its merits, and not only or chiefly for Philosophy, but also, and perhaps primarily, for the conduct of life. If he convinces men, should they need convincing, that they cannot be saved by the discursive reason alone, he will have done a good service to his generation, and to the philosophers among them who may (though they ought not to) be tempted to ignore the intuitive element in experience.

The same tendency to over-emphasis can be observed elsewhere. It is noticeable, for instance, in his discussions of Change, which are so marked and important a feature in his writings. His Philosophy has been called, with his approval apparently, the Philosophy of Change, though it might have been called, still more truly and suggestively, the Philosophy of Creation. It is this latter phase of it which has so enormously interested and stimulated the world. As to his treatment of Change, it reveals Bergson in one of his happiest moods. It is difficult to restrain one's praise in speaking of the subtle and resourceful way in which he handles this tantalizing and elusive question. It is a stroke of genius. The student of Philosophy, of course, at once thinks of Heraclitus; but Bergson is not merely another Heraclitus any more than he is just an echo of Jacobi. He places Change in a new light, enables us to grasp its character with a success which, if he had no other claim to remembrance, would ensure for him an honourable place in the History of Philosophy. In the process he makes but a mouthful of Zeno and his eternal puzzles. But, as Mr. Gunn also points out,[Footnote: See p. 142.] Change cannot be the last word in our characterization of Reality. Pure Change is not only unthinkable — that perhaps Bergson would allow — but it is something which cannot be experienced. There must be points of reference — a starting point and an ending point at least. Pure Change, as is the way with "pure" anything, turns into its contradictory. Paradoxical though it may seem, it ends as static. It becomes the One and Indivisible. This, at least, was recognized by Heraclitus and is expressed by him in his figure of the Great Year.

It is not my purpose, however, to usurp the function of the author of this useful handbook to Bergson. The extent of my introductory remarks is an almost involuntary tribute to the material and provocative nature of Bergson's discussions, just as the frequent use by the author of this book of the actual words of Bergson are a tribute to the excellence and essential rightness of his style. The Frenchman, himself a free and candid spirit, would be the last to require unquestioning docility in others. He knows that thereby is the philosophic breath choked out of us. If we read him in the spirit in which he would wish to be read, we shall find, however much we may diverge from him on particular issues, that our labour has been far from wasted. He undoubtedly calls for considerable effort from the student who takes him, as he ought to be taken, seriously; but it is effort well worth while. He, perhaps, shines even more as a psychologist than as a philosopher—at least in the time-honoured sense. He has an almost uncanny introspective insight and, as has been said, a power of rendering its result in language which creates in the reader a sense of excitement and adventure not to be excelled by the ablest romancer. Fadaises, which are to be met with in philosophical works as elsewhere, are not to be frequently encountered in his writings. There is always the fresh breeze of original thought blowing here. He is by nature as well as by doctrine the sworn foe of conventionality. Though he may not give us all we would wish, in our haste to be all-wise, let us yet be grateful to him for this, that he has the purpose and also the power to shake us out of complacency, to compel us to recast our philosophical account. In this he is supremely serviceable to his generation, and is deserving of the gratitude of all who care for Philosophy. For, while Philosophy cannot die, it may be allowed to fall into a comatose condition; and this is the unpardonable sin.

ALEXANDER MAIR

LIVERPOOL UNIVERSITY

This huge vision of time and motion, of a mighty world which is always becoming, always changing, growing, striving, and wherein the word of power is not law, but life, has captured the modern imagination no less than the modern intellect. It lights with its splendour the patient discoveries of science. It casts a new radiance on theology, ethics and art. It gives meaning to some of our deepest instincts, our strangest and least explicable tendencies. But above and beyond all this, it lifts the awful weight which determinism had laid upon our spirits and fills the future with hope; for beyond the struggle and suffering inseparable from life's flux, as we know it, it reports to us, though we may not hear them, "the thunder of new wings."

Evelyn Underhill

CHAPTER I
LIFE OF BERGSON

Birth and education—Teaches at Clermont-Ferrand—Les donnees immediates de la conscience—Matiere et Memoire—Chair of Greek Philosophy, then of Modern Philosophy, College de France—L'Evolution creatrice—Relations with William James—Visits England and America—Popularity—Neo-Catholics and Syndicalists—Election to Academie francaise—War-work—

L'Energie spirituelle.

Bergson's life has been the quiet and uneventful one of a French professor, the chief landmarks in it being the publication of his three principal works, first, in 1889, the Essai sur les donnees immediates de la conscience, then Matiere et Memoire in 1896, and L'Evolution creatrice in 1907. On October 18th, 1859, Henri Louis Bergson was born in Paris in the Rue Lamartine, not far from the Opera House.[Footnote: He was not born in England as Albert Steenbergen erroneously states in his work, Henri Bergsons Intuitive Philosophie, Jena, 1909, p. 2, nor in 1852, the date given by Miss Stebbing in her Pragmatism and French Voluntarism.] He is descended from a prominent Jewish family of Poland, with a blend of Irish blood from his mother's side. His family lived in London for a few years after his birth, and he obtained an early familiarity with the English language from his mother. Before he was nine years old his parents crossed the Channel and settled in France, Henri becoming a naturalized citizen of the Republic.

In Paris from 1868 to 1878 he attended the Lycee Fontaine, now known as the Lycee Condorcet. While there he obtained a prize for his scientific work and also won a prize when he was eighteen for the solution of a mathematical problem. This was in 1877, and his solution was published the following year in Annales de Mathematiques. It is of interest as being his first published work. After some hesitation over his career, as to whether it should lie in the sphere of the sciences or that of "the humanities," he decided in favour of the latter, and when nineteen years of age, he entered the famous Ecole Normale Superieure. While there he obtained the degree of

Licencie-es-Lettres, and this was followed by that of Agrege de philosophie in 1881.

The same year he received a teaching appointment at the Lycee in Angers, the ancient capital of Anjou. Two years later he settled at the Lycee Blaise-Pascal in Clermont-Ferrand, chief town of the Puy de Dome department, whose name is more known to motorists than to philosophers. The year after his arrival at Clermont-Ferrand he displayed his ability in "the humanities" by the publication of an excellent edition of extracts from Lucretius, with a critical study of the text and the philosophy of the poet (1884), a work whose repeated editions are sufficient evidence of its useful place in the promotion of classical study among the youth of France. While teaching and lecturing in this beautiful part of his country (the Auvergne region), Bergson found time for private study and original work. He was engaged on his Essai sur les donnees immediates de la conscience. This essay, which, in its English translation, bears the more definite and descriptive title, Time and Free Will, was submitted, along with a short Latin Thesis on Aristotle, for the degree of Docteur-es-Lettres, to which he was admitted by the University of Paris in 1889. The work was published in the same year by Felix Alcan, the Paris publisher, in his series La Bibliotheque de philosophie contemporaine.

It is interesting to note that Bergson dedicated this volume to Jules Lachelier, then ministre de l'instruction publique, who was an ardent disciple of Ravaisson and the author of a rather important philosophical work Du fondement de l'Induction (1871), who in his view of things endeavoured "to substitute everywhere force for inertia, life for death, and liberty for fatalism." [Footnote: Lachelier was born in 1832, Ravaisson in 1813. Bergson owed much to both of these teachers of the Ecole Normale Superieure. Cf. his memorial address on Ravaisson, who died in 1900. (See Bibliography under 1904.)]

Bergson now settled again in Paris, and after teaching for some months at the Municipal College, known as the College Rollin, he received an appointment at the Lycee Henri-Quatre, where he remained for eight years. In 1896 he published his second large work, entitled Matiere et Memoire. This rather difficult, but brilliant, work investigates the function of the brain, undertakes an analysis of perception and memory, leading up to a careful consideration of the problems of the relation of body and mind. Bergson, we know, has spent years of research in preparation for each of his three large works. This is especially obvious in Matiere et Memoire, where he shows a very thorough acquaintance with the extensive amount of pathological investigation which has been carried out in recent years, and for which France is justly entitled to very honourable mention.

In 1898 Bergson became Maitre de conferences at his Alma Mater, L'Ecole Normale Superieure, and was later promoted to a Professorship. The year 1900 saw him installed as Professor at the College de France, where he accepted the Chair of Greek Philosophy in succession to Charles L'Eveque. The College de France, founded in 1530, by Francois I, is less ancient, and until recent years has been less prominent in general repute than the Sorbonne, which traces back its history to the middle of the thirteenth century. Nevertheless, it is one of the intellectual headquarters of France, indeed of the whole world. While the Sorbonne is now the seat of the University of Paris, the College is an independent institution under the control of the Ministre de l'Instruction publique. The lectures given by the very eminent professors who fill its forty-three chairs are free and open to the general public, and are attended mainly by a large number of women students and by the senior students from the University. The largest lecture room in the College was given to Bergson, but this became quite inadequate to accommodate his hearers.

At the First International Congress of Philosophy, which was held in Paris, during the first five days of August, 1900, Bergson read a short, but important, paper, Sur les origines psychologiques de notre croyance a la loi de causalite. In 1901 Felix Alcan published in book form a work which had just previously appeared in the Revue de Paris entitled Le Rire, one of the most important of his minor productions. This essay on the meaning of the Comic was based on a lecture which he had given in his early days in the Auvergne. The study of it is essential to an understanding of Bergson's views of life, and its passages dealing with the place of the artistic in life are valuable. In 1901 he was elected to the Academie des Sciences morales et politiques, and became a member of the Institute. In 1903 he contributed to the Revue de metaphysique et de morale a very important essay entitled Introduction a la metaphysique, which is useful as a preface to the study of his three large books.

On the death of Gabriel Tarde, the eminent sociologist, in 1904, Bergson succeeded him in the Chair of Modern Philosophy. From the 4th to the 8th of September of that year he was at Geneva attending the Second International Congress of Philosophy, when he lectured on Le Paralogisme psycho-physiologique, or, to quote its new title, Le Cerveau et la Pensee: une illusion philosophique. An illness prevented his visiting Germany to attend the Third Congress held at Heidelberg.

His third large work—his greatest book—L'Evolution creatrice, appeared in 1907, and is undoubtedly, of all his works, the one which is most widely known and most discussed. It constitutes one of the most profound and original contributions to the philosophical consideration of the theory of Evolution. Un livre comme L'Evolution creatrice, remarks Imbart de la Tour, n'est pas seulment une oeuvre, mais une date, celle d'une direction nouvelle imprimee a la pensee. By 1918, Alcan, the publisher, had issued twenty-one editions, making an average of two editions per annum for ten years. Since the appearance of this book, Bergson's popularity has increased enormously, not only in academic circles, but among the general reading public.

He came to London in 1908 and visited William James, the American philosopher of Harvard, who was Bergson's senior by seventeen years, and who was instrumental in calling the attention of the Anglo-American public to the work of the French professor. This was an interesting meeting and we find James' impression of Bergson given in his Letters under date of October 4, 1908. "So modest and unpretending a man but such a genius intellectually! I have the strongest suspicions that the tendency which he has brought to a focus, will end by prevailing, and that the present epoch will be a sort of turning point in the history of philosophy."

As in some quarters erroneous ideas prevail regarding both the historical and intellectual relation between James and Bergson, it may be useful to call attention to some of the facts here. As early as 1880 James contributed an article in French to the periodical La Critique philosophique, of Renouvier and Pillon, entitled Le Sentiment de l'Effort.[Footnote: Cf. his Principles of Psychology, Vol. II., chap xxvi.] Four years later a couple of articles by him appeared in Mind: What is an Emotion?[Footnote: Mind, 1884, pp. 188-205.] and On some Omissions of Introspective Psychology. [Footnote: Mind, 1884, pp. 1-26.] Of these articles the first two were quoted by Bergson in his work of 1889, Les donnees immediates de la conscience. In the following years 1890-91 appeared the two volumes of James' monumental work, The Principles of Psychology, in which he refers to a pathological phenomenon observed by Bergson. Some writers taking merely these dates into consideration, and overlooking the fact that James' investigations had been proceeding since 1870, registered from time to time by various articles which culminated in The Principles, have mistakenly assigned to Bergson's ideas priority in time.[Footnote: For example A. Chaumeix: William James (Revue des Deux Mondes, Oct, 1910), and J. Bourdeau: Nouvelles modes en philosophie, Journal de Debats, Feb., 1907. Cf. Flournoy: La philosophie de William James. (Eng. Trans. Holt and James, pp. 198-206).] On the other hand insinuations have been made to the effect that Bergson owes the germ-ideas of his first book to the 1884 article by James On Some Omissions of Introspective Psychology, which he neither refers to nor quotes. This particular article deals with the conception of thought as a stream of consciousness, which intellect distorts by framing into concepts. We must not be misled by parallels. Bergson has replied to this insinuation by denying that he had any knowledge of the article by James when he wrote Les donnees immediates de la conscience.[Footnote: Relation a William James et a James Ward. Art. in Revue philosophique, Aug., 1905, lx., p. 229.] The two thinkers appear to have developed independently until almost the close of the century. In truth they are much further apart in their intellectual position than is frequently supposed.[Footnote: The reader who desires to follow the various views of the relation of Bergson and James will find the following works useful. Kallen (a pupil of James): William James and Henri Bergson: a study in contrasting theories of life. Stebbing: Pragmatism and French Voluntarism. Caldwell: Pragmatism and Idealism (last chap). Perry: Present Philosophical Tendencies. Boutroux: William James (Eng. Tr.). Flournoy: La philosophie de James (Eng. Tr.). And J. E. Turner: An Examination of William James' Philosophy.] Both have succeeded in appealing to audiences far beyond the purely academic sphere, but only in their mutual rejection of "intellectualism" as final is there real harmony or unanimity between them. It will not do to press too closely analogies between the Radical Empiricism of the American and the Doctrine of Intuition of the Frenchman. Although James obtains a certain priority in point of time in the development and enunciation of his ideas, we must remember that he confessed that he was baffled by many of Bergson's notions. James certainly neglected many of the deeper metaphysical aspects of Bergson's thought, which did not harmonize with his own, and are even in direct contradiction. In addition to this Bergson is no pragmatist, for him "utility," so far from being a test of truth, is rather the reverse, a synonym for error.

Nevertheless, William James hailed Bergson as an ally very enthusiastically. Early in the century (1903) we find him remarking in his correspondence: "I have been re-reading Bergson's books, and nothing that I have read since years has so excited and stimulated my thoughts. I am sure that that philosophy has a great future, it breaks through old cadres and brings things into a solution from which new crystals can be got." The most noteworthy tributes paid by him to Bergson were those made in the Hibbert Lectures (A Pluralistic Universe), which James gave at Manchester College, Oxford, shortly after he and Bergson met in London. He there remarked upon the encouragement he had received from Bergson's thought, and referred to the confidence he had in being "able to lean on Bergson's authority." [Footnote: A Pluralistic Universe, pp. 214-15. Cf. the whole of Lecture V. The Compounding of Consciousness, pp. 181-221, and Lecture VI. Bergson and His Critique of Intellectualism, pp. 225-273.] "Open Bergson, and new horizons loom on every page you read. It is like the breath of the morning and the song of birds. It tells of reality itself, instead of merely reiterating what dusty-minded professors have written about what other previous professors have thought. Nothing in Bergson is shop-worn or at second-hand." [Footnote: Lecture VI., p. 265.] The influence of Bergson had led him "to renounce the intellectualist method and the current notion that logic is an adequate measure of what can or cannot be." [Footnote: A Pluralistic Universe, p. 212.] It had induced him, he continued, "TO GIVE UP THE LOGIC, squarely and irrevocably" as a method, for he found that "reality, life, experience, concreteness, immediacy, use what word you will, exceeds our logic, overflows, and surrounds it." [Footnote: A Pluralistic Universe, p. 212.]

Naturally, these remarks, which appeared in book form in 1909, directed many English and American readers to an investigation of Bergson's philosophy for themselves. A certain handicap existed in that his greatest work had not then been translated into English. James, however, encouraged and assisted Dr. Arthur Mitchell in his preparation of the English translation of L'Evolution creatrice. In August of 1910 James died. It was his intention, had he lived to see the completion of the translation, to introduce it to the English reading public by a prefatory note of appreciation. In the following year the translation was completed and still greater interest in Bergson and his work was the result. By a coincidence, in that same year (1911), Bergson penned for the French translation of James' book, Pragmatism,[Footnote: Le Pragmatisme: Translated by Le Brun. Paris, Flammarion.] a preface of sixteen pages, entitled Verite et Realite. In it he expressed sympathetic appreciation of James' work, coupled with certain important reservations.

In April (5th to 11th) Bergson attended the Fourth International Congress of Philosophy held at Bologna, in Italy, where he gave a brilliant address on L'Intuition philosophique. In response to invitations received he came again to England in May of that year, and has paid us several subsequent visits. These visits have always been noteworthy events and have been marked by important deliverances. Many of these contain important contributions to thought and shed new light on many passages in his three large works, Time and Free Will, Matter and Memory, and Creative Evolution. Although necessarily brief statements, they are of more recent date than his books, and thus show how this acute thinker can develop and enrich his thought and take advantage of such an opportunity to make clear to an English audience the fundamental principles of his philosophy.

He visited Oxford and delivered at the University, on the 26th and 27th of May, two lectures entitled La Perception du Changement, which were published in French in the same year by the Clarendon Press. As Bergson has a delightful gift of lucid and brief exposition, when the occasion demands such treatment, these lectures on Change form a most valuable synopsis or brief survey of the fundamental principles of his thought, and serve the student or general reader alike as an excellent introduction to the study of the larger volumes. Oxford honoured its distinguished visitor by conferring upon him the degree of Doctor of Science. Two days later he delivered the Huxley Lecture at Birmingham University, taking for his subject Life and Consciousness. This subsequently appeared in The Hibbert Journal (Oct., 1911), and since revised, forms the first essay in the collected volume L'Energie spirituelle or Mind-Energy. In October he was again in England, where he had an enthusiastic reception, and delivered at London University (University College) four lectures on La Nature de l'Ame. In 1913 he visited the United States of America, at the invitation of Columbia University, New York, and lectured in several American cities, where he was welcomed by very large audiences. In February, at Columbia University, he lectured both in French and English, taking as his subjects: Spiritualite et Liberte and The Method of Philosophy. Being again in England in May of the same year, he accepted the Presidency of the British Society for Psychical Research, and delivered to the Society an impressive address: Fantomes des Vivants et Recherche psychique.

Meanwhile, his popularity increased, and translations of his works began to appear in a number of languages, English, German, Italian, Danish, Swedish, Magyar, Polish and Russian. In 1914 he was honoured by his fellow-countrymen in being elected as a member of the Academie francaise. He was also made President of the Academie des Sciences morales et politiques, and in addition he became Officier de la Legion d'Honneur, and Officier de l'Instruction publique. He found disciples of many varied types, and in France movements such as Neo-Catholicism or Modernism on the one hand and Syndicalism on the other, endeavoured to absorb and to appropriate for their own immediate use and propaganda some of the central ideas of his teaching. That important continental organ of socialist and syndicalist theory, Le Mouvement socialiste, suggested that the realism of Karl Marx and Prudhon is hostile to all forms of intellectualism, and that, therefore, supporters of Marxian socialism should welcome a philosophy such as that of Bergson. Other writers, in their eagerness, asserted the collaboration of the Chair of Philosophy at the College de France with the aims of the Confederation Generale du Travail and the Industrial Workers of the World. It was claimed that there is harmony between the flute of personal philosophical meditation and the trumpet of social revolution. These statements are considered in the chapter dealing with the political implications of Bergson's thought.

While social revolutionaries were endeavouring to make the most out of Bergson, many leaders of religious thought, particularly the more liberal-minded theologians of all creeds, e.g., the Modernists and Neo-Catholic Party in his own country, showed a keen interest in his writings, and many of them endeavoured to find encouragement and stimulus in his work. The Roman Catholic Church, however, which still believes that finality was reached in philosophy with the work of Thomas Aquinas, in the thirteenth century, and consequently makes that mediaeval philosophy her official, orthodox, and dogmatic view, took the step of banning Bergson's three books by placing them upon the Index (Decree of June 1, 1914).

It was arranged by the Scottish Universities that Bergson should deliver in 1914 the famous Gifford Lectures, and one course was planned for the spring and another for the autumn. The first course, consisting of eleven lectures, under the title of The Problem of Personality, was delivered at Edinburgh University in the Spring of that year.

Then came the War. The course of lectures planned for the autumn months had to be abandoned. Bergson has not, however, been silent during the conflict, and he has given some inspiring addresses. As early as November 4th, 1914, he wrote an article entitled La force qui s'use et celle qui ne s'use pas, which appeared in that unique and interesting periodical of the poilus, Le Bulletin des Armees de la Republique Francaise. A presidential address delivered in December, 1914, to the Academie des sciences morales et politiques, had for its title La Significance de la Guerre. This, together with the preceding article, has been translated and published in England as The Meaning of the War. Bergson contributed also to the publication arranged by The Daily Telegraph in honour of the King of the Belgians, King Albert's Book (Christmas, 1914). In 1915 he was succeeded in the office of President of the Academie des Sciences morales et politiques by M. Alexandre Ribot, and then delivered a discourse on The Evolution of German Imperialism. Meanwhile he found time to issue at the request of the Minister of Public Instruction a delightful little summary of French Philosophy. Bergson did a large amount of travelling and lecturing in America during the war. He was there when the French Mission under M. Viviani paid a visit in April and

May of 1917, following upon America's entry into the conflict. M. Viviani's book La Mission francaise en Amerique, 1917, contains a preface by Bergson.

Early in 1918 he was officially received by the Academie francaise, taking his seat among "The Select Forty" as successor to M. Emile Ollivier, the author of the large and notable historical work L'Empire liberal. A session was held in January in his honour at which he delivered an address on Ollivier.

In the War, Bergson saw the conflict of Mind and Matter, or rather of Life and Mechanism; and thus he shows us in action the central idea of his own philosophy. To no other philosopher has it fallen, during his lifetime, to have his philosophical principles so vividly and so terribly tested. We are too close to the smoking crucible of war to be aware of all that has been involved in it. Even those who have helped in the making of history are too near to it to regard it historically, much less philosophically. Yet one cannot help feeling that the defeat of German militarism has been the proof in action of the validity of much of Bergson's thought.

As many of Bergson's contributions to French periodicals are not readily accessible, he agreed to the request of his friends that these should be collected and published in two volumes. The first of these was being planned when war broke out. The conclusion of strife has been marked by the appearance of this delayed volume in 1919. It bears the title L'Energie spirituelle: Essais et Conferences. The noted expounder of Bergson's philosophy in England, Dr. Wildon Carr, has prepared an English Translation under the title Mind-Energy. The volume opens with the Huxley Memorial Lecture of 1911, Life and Consciousness, in a revised and developed form under the title Consciousness and Life. Signs of Bergson's growing interest in social ethics and in the idea of a future life of personal survival are manifested. The lecture before the Society for Psychical Research is included, as is also the one given in France, L'Ame et le Corps, which contains the substance of the four London lectures on the Soul. The seventh and last article is a reprint of Bergson's famous lecture to the Congress of Philosophy at Geneva in 1904, Le paralogisme psycho-physiologique, which now appears as Le Cerveau et la Pensee: une illusion philosophique. Other articles are on the False Recognition, on Dreams, and Intellectual Effort. The volume is a most welcome production and serves to bring together what Bergson has written on the concept of mental force, and on his view of "tension" and "detension" as applied to the relation of matter and mind.

It is Bergson's intention to follow up this collection shortly by another on the Method of Philosophy, dealing with the problems of

Intuition. For this he is preparing an important introduction, dealing with recent developments in philosophy. This second volume will include the Lectures on The Perception of Change given at Oxford, The Introduction to Metaphysics, and the brilliant paper Philosophical Intuition. In June, 1920, Cambridge honoured him with the degree of Doctor of Letters. In order that he may be able to devote his full time to the great new work he is preparing on ethics, religion, and sociology, Bergson has been relieved of the duties attached to the Chair of Modern Philosophy at the College de France. He still holds this chair, but no longer delivers lectures, his place being taken by his brilliant pupil Edouard Le Roy. Living with his wife and daughter in a modest house in a quiet street near the Porte d'Auteuil in Paris, Bergson is now working as keenly and vigorously as ever.

CHAPTER II
THE REALITY OF CHANGE

Fundamental in Bergson's philosophy. We are surrounded by changes—we ourselves change—Belief in change—Simplicity of change—Immobility is composite and relative—All movement is indivisible. The fallacy of "states"—Intellect loves the static—Life is dynamic—Change, the very stuff of life, constitutes reality.

Throughout the history of thought we find that the prevailing philosophies have always reflected some of the characteristics of their time. For instance, in those periods when, as historians tell us, the tendency towards unity, conformity, system, order, and authority was strong, we find philosophy reflecting these conditions by emphasizing the unity of the universe; while in those periods in which established order, system, and authority were disturbed, the philosophy of the time emphasizes the idea of multiplicity as opposed to the unity of the universe, laying stress on freedom, creative action, spontaneity of effort, and the reality of change. There can be little doubt that this is the chief reason why Bergson's philosophy has found such an amount of acceptance in a comparatively short period. The response to his thought may be explained very largely by this, that already his fundamental ideas existed, although implicit, unexpressed, in the minds of a great multitude of thoughtful people, to whom the static conceptions of the universe were inadequate and false.

We must not, on the other hand, overlook the fact that Bergson's statements have in their turn given an emphasis to all aspects of thought which take account of the reality of change and which realize its importance in all spheres. A writer on world politics very aptly reminds us that "life is change, and a League of Peace that aimed at preserving peace by forbidding change would be a tyranny as oppressive as any Napoleonic dictatorship. These problems called for periodic change. The peril of our future is that, while the need for change is instinctively grasped by some peoples as the fundamental fact of world-politics, to perceive it costs others a difficult effort of thought." [Footnote: H. N. Brailsford on Peace and Change, Chap. 3 of his Book A League of Nations.] However difficult it may be for some individuals and for some nations to grasp it, the great fact is there — the reality of change is undeniable.

Bergson himself would give to his philosophy the title, The Philosophy of Change, and this for a very good reason, for the principle of Change and an insistence on its reality lies at the root of his thought.[Footnote: He suggested this as a sub-title to Dr. H. Wildon Carr for his little work Henri Bergson (People's Books). Dr. Wildon Carr's later and larger work bears this as its full title.] "We know that everything changes," we find him saying in his London lectures, "but it is mere words. From the earliest times recorded in the history of philosophy, philosophers have never stopped saying that everything changes; but, when the moment came for the practical application of this proposition, they acted as if they believed that at the bottom of things there is immobility and invariability. The greatest difficulties of philosophy are due to not taking account of the fact that Change and Movement are universal. It is not enough to say that everything changes and moves — we must believe it." [Footnote: Second of the four lectures on La Nature de l'Ame delivered at London University, Oct. 21, 1911. From report in The Times for Oct. 23, 1911, p. 4.] In order to think Change and to see it, a whole mass of prejudices must be swept aside — some artificial, the products of speculative philosophy, and others the natural product of common-sense. We tend to regard immobility as a more simple affair than movement. But what we call immobility is really composite and is merely relative, being a relation between movements. If, for example, there are two trains running in the same direction on parallel lines at exactly the same speed, opposite one another, then the passengers in each train, when observing the other train, will regard the trains as motionless. So, generally, immobility is only apparent, Change is real. We tend to be misled by language; we speak, for instance, of 'the state of things'; but what we call a state is the appearance which a change assumes in the eyes of a being who, himself, changes according to an identical or analogous rhythm. "Take, for example," says Bergson, "a summer day. We are stretched on the grass, we look around us — everything is at rest — there is absolute immobility — no change. But the grass is growing, the leaves of the trees are developing or decaying — we ourselves are growing older all the time. That which seems rest, simplicity itself, is but a composite of our ageing with the changes which takes place in the grass, in the leaves, in all that is around us. Change, then, is simple, while 'the state of things' as we call it, is composite. Every stable state is the result of the co-existence between that change and the change of the person who perceives it." [Footnote: La Nature de l'Ame, lecture 2.]

It is an axiom in the philosophy of Bergson that all change or movement is indivisible. He asserts this expressly in Matter and Memory,[Footnote:

Matter and Memory, p. 246 ff. (Fr. p. 207 ff).] and again in the second lecture on The Perception of Change he deals with the indivisibility of movement somewhat fully, submitting it to a careful analysis, from which the following quotation is an extract—"My hand is at the point A. I move it to the point B, traversing the interval AB. I say that this movement from A to B is a simple thing—each of us has the sensation of this, direct and immediate. Doubtless, while we carry our hand over from A to B, we say to ourselves that we could stop it at an intermediate point, but then that would no longer be the same movement. There would then be two movements, with an interval of rest. Neither from within, by the muscular sense, nor from without, by sight, should we have the same perception. If we leave our movement from A to B such as it is, we feel it undivided, and we must declare it indivisible. It is true that when I look at my hand, going from A to B, traversing the interval AB, I say to myself 'the interval AB can be divided into as many parts as I wish, therefore the movement from A to B can be divided into as many parts as I like, since this movement covers this interval,' or, again, 'At each moment of its passing, the moving object passes over a certain point, therefore we can distinguish in the movement as many stopping-places as we wish—therefore the movement is infinitely divisible.' But let us reflect on this for a minute. How can the movement possibly coincide with the space which it traverses? How can the moving coincide with the motionless? How can the object which moves be said to 'be' at any point in its path? It passes over, or, in other words, it could 'be' there. It would 'be' there if it stopped there, but, if it stopped there, it is no longer the same movement with which we are dealing. It is always at one bound that a trajectory is traversed when, on its course, there is no stoppage. The bound may last a few seconds, or it may last for weeks, months, or years, but it is unique and cannot be decomposed. Only, when once the passage has been made, as the path is in space, and space is infinitely divisible, we picture to ourselves the movement itself as infinitely divisible. We like to imagine it thus, because, in a movement it is not the change of position which interests us, it is the positions themselves which the moving object has left, which it will take up, which it might assume if it were to stop in its course. We have need of immobility, and the more we succeed in presenting to ourselves the movement as coinciding with the space which it traverses, the better we think we understand it. Really, there is no true immobility, if we imply by that, an absence of movement." [Footnote: Translated from La Perception du Changement, pp. 19-20.] This immobility of which we have need for the purposes of action and of practical life, we erect into an absolute reality. It is of course convenient to our sense of sight to lay hold of objects in this way; as pioneer of the sense of touch, it prepares our action on the external world. But, although for all practical purposes we require the notion of immobility as part of our mental equipment, it does not at all help us to grasp reality. Then we habitually regard movement as something superadded to the motionless. This is quite legitimate in the world of affairs; but when we bring this habit into the world of speculation, we misconceive reality, we create lightheartedly insoluble problems, and close our eyes to what is most alive in the real world. For us movement is one position, then another position, and so on indefinitely. It is true that we say there must be something else, viz., the actual passing across the interval which separates those positions. But such a conception of Change is quite false. All true change or movement is indivisible. We, by constructing fictitious states and trying to compose movement out of them, endeavour to make a process coincide with a thing — a movement with an immobility. This is the way to arrive at dilemmas, antinomies, and blind-alleys of thought. The puzzles of Zeno about "Achilles and the Tortoise" and "The Moving Arrow" are classical examples of the error involved in treating movement as divisible.[Footnote: Bergson in Matter and Memory examines Zeno's four puzzles: "The Dichotomy," "Achilles and the Tortoise," "The Arrow" and "The Stadium."] If movement is not everything, it is nothing, and if we postulate, to begin with, that the motionless is real, then we shall be incapable of grasping reality. The philosophies of Plato, of Aristotle, and of Plotinus were developed from the thesis that there is more in the immutable than in the moving, and that it is by way of diminution that we pass from the stable to the unstable.

The main reason why it is such a difficult matter for us to grasp the reality of continuous change is owing to the limitations of our intellectual nature. "We are made in order to act, as much as and more than in order to think — or, rather, when we follow the bent of our nature, it is in order to act that we think." [Footnote: Creative Evolution, p. 313 (Fr. p. 321).] Intellect is always trying to carve out for itself stable forms because it is primarily fitted for action, and "is characterized by a natural inability to comprehend life" and grasp Change.[Footnote: Creative Evolution, p. 174 (Fr. p. 179).] Our intellect loves the solid and the static, but life itself is not static — it is dynamic. We might say that the intellect takes views across the ever-moving scene, snapshots of reality. It acts like the camera of the cinematograph operator, which is capable only of producing photographs, successive and static, in a series upon a ribbon. To grasp reality, we have to do what the cinematograph does with the film — that is, introduce or rather, re-introduce movement.[Footnote: Creative Evolution, pp. 320-324 (Fr. pp. 328-332).] The stiff photograph is an abstraction bereft of movement, so, too, our intellectual views of the world and of our own nature are static instead of being dynamic. Human life is not made up of childhood, adolescence, manhood, and old age as "states," although we tend to speak of it in this way. Life is not a thing, nor the state of a thing—it is a continuous movement or change. The soul itself is a movement, not an entity. In the physical world, light, when examined, proves itself to be a movement. Even physical science, bound, as it would seem, to assert the fixity and rigidity of matter, is now of the opinion that matter is not the solid thing we are apt to think it. The experiments of Kelvin and Lodge and the discovery of radium, have brought forward a new theory of matter; the old-fashioned base, the atom, is now regarded as being essentially movement; matter is as wonderful and mysterious in its character as spirit. Further we must note that the researches of Einstein, culminating in the formulation of his general Theory of Relativity and his special Theory of Gravitation, which are arousing such interest at the present time, threaten very seriously the older static views of the universe and seem to frustrate any efforts to find and denote any stability therein.[Footnote: Consult on this Dr. Einstein's own work of which the translation by R. W. Lawson is just published: Relativity: The Special and the General Theory. Methuen, 1920.] In the light of these discoveries, Bergson's views on the reality of Change seem less paradoxical than they might formerly have appeared. The reality of Change is, for Bergson, absolute, and on this, as a fundamental point, he constructs his thought. In conjunction with his study of Memory, it leads up to his discussions of Real Time (la duree), of Freedom, and of Creative Evolution. We must then, at the outset of any study of Bergson's philosophy, obtain a grasp of this universal 'becoming'—a vision of the reality of Change. Then we shall realize that Change is substantial, that it constitutes the very stuff of life. "There are changes, but there are not things that change; change does not need a support. There are movements, but there are not, necessarily, constant objects which are moved; movement does not imply something that is movable." [Footnote: Translated from La Perception du Changement, Lecture 2, p. 24.]

To emphasize and to illustrate this point, so fundamental in his thought, Bergson turns to music. "Let us listen," he says, "to a melody, letting ourselves be swayed by it; do we not have the clear perception of a movement which is not attached to any mobility—of a change devoid of anything which changes? The change is self-sufficient, it is the thing itself. It avails nothing to say that it takes time, for it is indivisible; if the melody were to stop sooner, it would not be any longer the same volume of sound, but another, equally indivisible. Doubtless we have a tendency to divide it and to represent it to ourselves as a linking together of distinct notes instead of the uninterrupted continuity of the melody. But why? Simply because our auditive perception has assumed the habit of saturating itself with visual images. We hear the melody across the vision which the conductor of the orchestra can have of it in looking at his score. We represent to ourselves notes linked on to notes on an imaginary sheet of paper. We think of a keyboard on which one plays, of the bow of a violin which comes and goes, of the musicians, each one of whom plays his part in conjunction with the others. Let us abstract these spatial images; there remains pure change, self-sufficing, in no way attached to a 'thing' which changes." [Footnote: Translated from La Perception du Changement, pp. 24-25.]

We must conceive reality as a continual flux, then immobility will seem a superficial abstraction hypostatized into states, concepts, and substances, and the old difficulties raised by the ancients, in regard to the problem of Change, will vanish, along with the problems attached to the notion of "substance" in modern thought, because there is nothing substantial but Change. Apart from Change there is no reality. We shall see that all is movement, that we ourselves are movement—part of an elan, a poussee formidable, which carries with it all things and all creatures, and that in this eternity—not of immutability but of life and Change—"we live and move and have our being." [Footnote: La Perception du Changement, concluding paragraph, p. 37.]

CHAPTER III
PERCEPTION

Images as data—Nerves, afferent and efferent, cannot beget images, nor can the brain give rise to representations—All our perception relative to action. Denial of this involves the fallacies of Idealism or of Realism—Perception and knowledge—Physiological data—Zone of indetermination—"Pure" perception—Memory and Perception.

From the study of Change we are led on to a consideration of the problems connected with our perception of the external world, which has its roots in change. These problems have given rise to some very opposing views—the classic warfare between Realism and Idealism. Bergson is of neither school, but holds that they each rest on misconceptions, a wrong emphasis on certain facts. He invites us to follow him closely while he investigates the problems of Perception in his own way.

"We will assume for the moment that we know nothing of theories of matter and theories of spirit, nothing of the discussions as to the reality or ideality of the external world. Here I am in the presence of images, in the vaguest sense of the word, images perceived when my senses are opened to them, unperceived when they are closed. ... Now of these images there is ONE which is distinct from all the others, in that I do not know it only from without by perceptions, but from within by affections; it is my body." [Footnote: Matter and Memory, p. 1 (Fr. p. 1).] Further examination shows me that these affections "always interpose themselves between the excitations from without and the movement which I am about to execute." [Footnote: Matter and Memory, p. 1 (Fr. p. 1).] Indeed all seems to take place as if, in this aggregate of images which I call the universe, nothing really new could happen except through the medium of certain particular images, the type of which is furnished me by my body." [Footnote: Matter and Memory, p. 3 (Fr. p. 2).] Reference to physiology shows in the structure of human bodies afferent nerves which transmit a disturbance to nerve centres, and also efferent nerves which conduct from other centres movement to the periphery, thus setting in motion the body in whole or in part. When we make enquiries from the physiologist or the psychologist with regard to the origin of these images and representations, we are sometimes told that, as the centrifugal movements of the nervous system can evoke movement of the body, so the centripetal movements — at least some of them — give rise to the representation, mental picture, or perception of the external world. Yet we must remember that the brain, the nerves, and the disturbance of the nerves are, after all, only images among others. So it is absurd to state that one image, say the brain, begets the others, for "the brain is part of the material world, but the material world is not part of the brain." Eliminate the image which bears the name 'material world,' and you destroy, at the same time, the brain and the cerebral disturbances which are parts of it. Suppose, on the contrary, that these two images, the brain and the cerebral disturbance, vanish; ex hypothesi you efface only these, that is to say, very little — an insignificant detail from an immense picture — the picture in its totality, that is to say, the whole universe remains. To make of the brain the condition on which the whole image depends is a contradiction in terms, since the brain is, by hypothesis, a part of this image." [Footnote: Matter and Memory, p. 4 (Fr. pp. 3-4).] The data of perception are external images, then my body, and changes brought about by my body in the surrounding images. The external images transmit movement to my body, it gives back movement to them. My body or part of my body, i.e., my brain, could not beget a whole or part of my representation of the external world. "You may say that my body is matter or that it is an image — the word is of no importance. If it is matter, it is a part of the material world, and the material world consequently exists around it and without it. If it is an image — that image can give but what has been put into it, and since it is, by hypothesis, the image of my body only, it would be absurd to expect to get from it that of the whole universe. My body, an object destined to move other objects, is then a centre of action; it cannot give birth to a representation." [Footnote: Matter and Memory, p. 5 (Fr. p. 4).] The body, however, is privileged, since it appears to choose within certain limits certain reactions from possible ones. It exercises a real influence on other images, deciding which step to take among several which may be possible. It judges which course is advantageous or dangerous to itself, by the nature of the images which reach it. The objects which surround my body reflect its possible action upon them. All our perception has reference, primarily, to action, not to speculation.[Footnote: Cf. Creative Evolution, p. 313 (Fr. p. 321).] The brain centres are concerned with motor reaction rather than with conscious perception, "the brain is an instrument of action and not of representation." [Footnote: Matter and Memory, p. 83 (Fr. p. 69).] Therefore, in the study of the problems of perception, the starting-point should be action and not sensation. All the confusions, inconsistencies and absurdities of statement, made in regard to our knowledge of the external world, have here their origin. Many philosophers and psychologists "show us a brain, analogous in its essence to the rest of the material universe, consequently an image, if the universe is an image. Then, since they want the internal movements of this brain to create or determine the representation of the whole material world — an image infinitely greater than that of the cerebral vibrations — they maintain that these molecular movements, and movement in general, are not images like others, but something which is either more or less than an image — in any case is of another nature than an image — and from which representation will issue as by a miracle. Thus matter is made into something radically different from representation, something of which, consequently, we have no image; over against it they place a consciousness empty of images, of which we are unable to form any idea. Lastly, to fill consciousness, they invent an incomprehensible action of this formless matter upon this matterless thought." [Footnote: Matter and Memory, p. 9 (Fr. pp. 7-8).]

The problem at issue between Realists and Idealists turns on the fact that there are two systems of images in existence. "Here is a system of images which I term 'my perception of the universe,' and which may be entirely altered by a very slight change in the privileged image — my body. This image occupies the centre. By it all the others are conditioned; at each of its movements everything changes as though by a turn of a kaleidoscope. Here, on the other hand, are the same images, but referred each one to itself, influencing each other no doubt, but in such a manner that the effect is always in proportion to the cause; this is what I term the 'universe.'" [Footnote: Matter and Memory, p. 12 (Fr. p. 10).] The question is, "How is it that the same images can belong at the same time to two different systems — the one in which each image varies for itself and in the well-defined measure that it is patient of the real action of surrounding images — the other in which all change for a single image and in the varying measure that they reflect the eventual action of this privileged image?" [Footnote: Matter and Memory, p. 13 (Fr. p. 11).] We may style one the system of science, the other the system of consciousness. Now, Realism and Idealism are both incapable of explaining why there are two such systems at all. Subjective Idealism derives the system of science from that of consciousness, while materialistic Realism derives the system of consciousness from that of science. They have, however, this common meeting-place, that they both regard Perception as speculative in character — for each of them "to perceive" is to "know." Now this is just the postulate which Bergson disputes. The office of perception, according to him, is to give us, not knowledge, but the conditions necessary for action.[Footnote: Notre croyance a la loi de causalite (Revue de metaphysique et de morale, 1900), p. 658.] A little examination shows us that distance stands for the degree in which other bodies are protected, as it were, against the action of my body against them, and equally too for the degree in which my body is protected from them.[Footnote: Le Souvenir du present et la fausse reconnaissance in L'Energie spirituelle, pp. 117-161 (Mind-Energy), or Revue philosophique, 1908, pp. 561-593.] Perception is utilitarian in character and has reference to bodily action, and we detach from all the images coming to us those which interest us practically.

Bergson then examines the physiological aspects of the perceptual process. Beginning with reflex actions and the development of the nervous system, he goes on to discuss the functions of the spinal cord and the brain. He finds in regard to these last two that "there is only a difference of degree — there can be no difference in kind — between what is called the perceptive faculty of the brain and the reflex functions of the spinal cord. The cord transforms into movements the stimulation received, the brain prolongs into reactions which are merely nascent, but in the one case as in the other, the function of the nerve substance is to conduct, to co-ordinate, or to inhibit movements.[Footnote: Matter and Memory, pp. 10-11 (Fr. p. 9).] As we rise in the organic series we find a division of physiological labour. Nerve cells appear, are diversified and tend to group themselves into a system; at the same time the animal reacts by more varied movements to external stimulation. But even when the stimulation received is not at once prolonged into movement, it appears merely to await its occasion; and the same impression which makes the organism aware of changes in the environment, determines it or prepares it to adapt itself to them. No doubt there is in the higher vertebrates a radical distinction between pure automatism, of which the seat is mainly in the spinal cord, and voluntary activity which requires the intervention of the brain. It might be imagined that the impression received, instead of expanding into more movements spiritualizes itself into consciousness. But as soon as we compare the structure of the spinal cord with that of the brain, we are bound to infer that there is merely a difference of complication, and not a difference in kind, between the functions of the brain and the reflex activity of the medullary system." [Footnote: Matter and Memory, pp. 17-18 (Fr. p. 15).] The brain is no more than a kind of central telephone exchange, its office is to allow communication or to delay it. It adds nothing to what it receives, it is simply a centre where perceptions get into touch with motor mechanisms. Sometimes the function of the brain is to conduct the movement received to a chosen organ of reaction, while at other times it opens to the movement the totality of the motor tracks. The brain appears as an instrument of analysis in regard to movements received by it, but an instrument of selection in regard to the movements executed. In either case, its office is limited to the transmission and division of movements. In the lower organisms, stimulation takes the form of immediate contact. For example, a jelly-fish feels a danger when anything touches it, and reacts immediately. The more immediate the reaction has to be, the more it resembles simple contact. Higher up the scale, sight and hearing enable the individual to enter into relation with a greater number of objects and with objects at a distance. This gives rise to an amount of uncertainty, "a zone of indetermination," where hesitation and choice come into play. Hence, says Bergson: "Perception is master of space in the exact measure in which action is master of time." [Footnote: Matter and Memory, p. 23 (Fr. p. 19).]

In the paper read before the First International Congress of Philosophy at Paris in 1900, on Our Belief in the Law of Causality,[Footnote: Notre croyance a la loi de causalite (Revue de metaphysique et de morale, Sept., 1900, pp. 655-660).] Bergson showed that it has its root in the co-ordination of our tactile impressions with our visual impressions. This co-ordination becomes a continuity which generates motor habits or tendencies to action.

There now comes up for consideration the question as to why this relation of the organism, to more or less distinct objects, takes the particular form of conscious perception, and further, why does everything happen as if this consciousness were born of the internal movements of the cerebral substance? To answer this question, we must turn to perceptual processes, as these occur in our everyday life. We find at once that "there is no perception which is not full of memories. With the immediate and present data of our senses, we mingle a thousand details out of our past experience." [Footnote: Matter and Memory, p. 24 (Fr. p. 20).] To such an extent is this true that the immediate data of perception serve as a sign to bring much more to the mind. Psychological experiments have conclusively proved that we never actually perceive all that we imagine to be there. Hence arise illusions, examples of which may be easily thought of — incorrect proof-reading is one, while another common one is the mistake of taking one person for another because of some similarity of dress. What is actually perceived is but a fraction of what we are looking at and acts normally as a suggestion for the whole. Now, although it is true that, in practice, Perception and Memory are never found absolutely separate in their purity, yet it is necessary to distinguish them from one another absolutely in any investigation of a psychological nature. If, instead of a perception impregnated with memory-images, nothing survived from the past, then we should have "pure" perception, not coloured by anything in the individual's past history, and so a kind of impersonal perception. However unreal it may seem, such a perception is at the root of our knowledge of things and individual accidents are merely grafted on to this impersonal or "pure" perception. Just because philosophers have overlooked it, and because they have failed to distinguish it from that which memory contributes to it, they have regarded Perception as a kind of interior and subjective vision, differing from Memory only by its greater intensity and not differing in nature. In reality, however, Perception and Memory differ fundamentally.

Our conscious perception is just our power of choice, reflected from things as though by a mirror, so that representation arises from the omission of that in the totality of matter which has no bearing on our needs and consequently no interest for us. "There is for images merely a difference of degree and not of kind between 'being' and 'being consciously perceived.'" [Footnote: Matter and Memory, p. 30 (Fr. p. 25).] Consciousness — in regard to external perception — is explained by this indeterminateness and this choice. "But there is in this necessary poverty of conscious perception, something that is positive, that foretells spirit; it is, in the etymological sense of the word, discernment.'" [Footnote: Matter and Memory, p. 31 (Fr. p. 26).] The chief difficulty in dealing with the problems of Perception, is to explain "not how Perception arises, but how it is limited, since it should be the image of the whole and is in fact reduced to the image of that which interests you." [Footnote: Matter and Memory, p. 34 (Fr. p. 29).] We only make an insuperable difficulty if we imagine Perception to be a kind of photographic view of things, taken from a fixed point by that special apparatus which is called an organ of perception — a photograph which would then be developed in the brain-matter by some unknown chemical and psychical process. "Everything happens as though your perception were a result of the internal motions of the brain and issued in some sort from the cortical centres. It could not actually come from them since the brain is an image like others, enveloped in the mass of other images, and it would be absurd that the container should issue from the content. But since the structure of the brain is like the detailed plan of the movements among which you have the choice, and since that part of the external images which appears to return upon itself, in order to constitute perception, includes precisely all the points of the universe which these movements could affect, conscious perception and cerebral movement are in strict correspondence. The reciprocal dependence of these two terms is therefore simply due to the fact that both are functions of a third, which is the indetermination of the Will." [Footnote: Matter and Memory, p. 35 (Fr. p. 29).]

Moreover, we must recognize that the image is formed and perceived in the object, not in the brain, even although it would seem that rays of light coming from a point P are perceived along the path of the sensori-motor processes in the brain and are afterwards projected into P. There is not, however, an unextended image which forms itself in consciousness and then projects itself into the position P. Really, the point P, and the rays which it emits, together with the retina and nervous elements affected in the process of perception, all form a single whole. The point P is an indispensable factor in this whole and it is really in P and not anywhere else that the image of P is formed and perceived.[Footnote: Cf. Matter and Memory, p. 37 (Fr p. 31), also paper entitled Notre croyance a la loi de causalite in the Revue de metaphysique et de morale, 1900, p. 658.]

In the field of "pure" perception, that is to say, perception unadulterated by the addition of memory-images, there can arise no image without an object. "Sensation is essentially due to what is actually present." [Footnote: Le Souvenir du present et la fausse reconnaissance, p. 579 of Revue philosophique, Dec., 1908; also L'Energie spirituelle, p. 141 (Mind-Energy).] Exactly how external stimuli, such as rays of a certain speed and length, come to give us a certain image, e.g., the sensation "red" or the sound of "middle C," we shall never understand. "No trace of the movements themselves can be actually perceived in the sensation which translates them." [Footnote: Time and Free Will, pp. 34-35 (Fr. p. 26).] We only make trouble by regarding sensations in an isolated manner and attempting to construct Perception from them. "Our sensations are to our perceptions, that which the real action of our body is to its possible or virtual action." [Footnote: Matter and Memory, p. 58 (Fr. p. 48).] Thus, everything happens as if the external images were reflected by our body into surrounding space. This is why the surface of the body, which forms the common limit of the external and internal, is the only portion of space which is both perceived and felt. Just as external objects are perceived by me where they are, in themselves and not in me, so my affective states (e.g. pains—which are local, unavailing efforts) are experienced where they occur, in my body. Consider the system of images which we term the "external world." My body is one of them and around it is grouped the representation, i.e., its eventual influence on others. Within it occurs affection, i.e., its actual effort upon itself. It is because of this distinction between images and sensations that we affirm that the totality of perceived images subsists, even if our body disappears, whereas we cannot annihilate our body without destroying our sensations. In practice, our "pure" perception is adulterated with affection, as well as with memories. To understand Perception, however, we must— as previously insisted upon—study it with reference to action. It is false to suppose "that perception and sensation exist for their own sake; the philosopher ascribes to them an entirely speculative function," [Footnote: Matter and Memory, p. 311 (Fr p. 261).] a proceeding which gives rise to the fallacies of Realism and Idealism.

It has been said that the choice of perceptions from among images in general is the effect of a "discernment" which foreshadows spirit. But to touch the reality of spirit, we must place ourselves at the point where an individual consciousness continues and retains the past in a present, enriched by it.[Footnote: See Chapter VI on la duree. Time—True and False.] Perception we never meet in its pure state; it is always mingled with memories. The rose has a different scent for you from that which it has for me, just because the scent of the rose bears with it all the memories of all the roses we have ever experienced, each of us individually.[Footnote: Time and Free Will, pp. 161-162 (Fr. p. 124).] Memory, however mingled with Perception, is nevertheless fundamentally different in character.[Footnote: Le Souvenir du present et la fausse reconnaissance, Revue philosophique, Dec., 1908, p. 580; also L'Effort intellectuel, Revue philosophique, Jan., 1902, p. 23; L'Energie spirituelle, pp. 141 and 197 (Mind-Energy).] "When we pass from 'pure' Perception to Memory, we definitely abandon matter for spirit." [Footnote: Matter and Memory, p. 313 (Fr. p. 263).]

CHAPTER IV
MEMORY

Definition — Two forms — memorizing power related to habit; recalling power or "pure" memory. Is memory a function of the brain? — Pathological Phenomena. Memory something other than merely a function of the brain. The "Box" theory — Memory records everything — Dreams — The well-balanced mind — Memory a manifestation of spirit.

The importance of Memory is recognized by all persons — whether psychologists or not. At the present time there is a growing interest in systems of memory-training offered to the public, which aim at mental efficiency as a means to success in life. Indeed, from the tone of some advertisements seen in the press, one might be prompted to think that Memory itself was the sole factor determining success in either a professional or a business career. Yet, although we are likely to regard this as a somewhat exaggerated statement, nevertheless we cannot deny the very great importance of the power of Memory. How often, in everyday life, we hear people excuse themselves by remarking "My memory failed me" or "played me false" or, more bluntly, "I forgot all about that." Without doubt, Memory is a most vital factor, though not the only one in mental efficiency.[Footnote: The true ideal of mental efficiency must include power of Will as well as of Memory.] It is an element in mental life which puzzles both the specialist in psychology and the layman. "What is this wonderfully subtle power of mind?" "How do we remember?" Even the mind, untrained in psychological investigation, cannot help asking such questions in moments of reflection; but for the psychologist they are questions of very vital significance in his science. For Bergson, as psychologist, Memory is naturally, a subject of great importance. We must note, however, that for Bergson, as metaphysician, it plays an even more important role, since his study of Memory and conclusions as to its nature lead him on to a discussion of the relation of soul and body, spirit and matter. His second large work, which appeared in 1896, bears the title Matiere et Memoire. For him, Memory is a pivot on which turns a whole scheme of relationships — material and spiritual. He wrote in 1910 a new introduction for the English Translation of this work. He there says that "among all the facts capable of throwing light on the psycho-physiological relation, those which concern Memory, whether in the normal or the pathological state, hold a privileged position." [Footnote: Introduction to Matter and Memory, p. xii.] Let us then, prior to passing on to the consideration of the problem of the relation of soul and body, examine what Bergson has to say on the subject of Memory.

At the outset, we may define Memory as the return to consciousness of some experience, accompanied by the awareness that it has been present earlier at a definite time and place.[Footnote: The above is to be taken as a definition of the normal memory. In a subtle psychological analysis in the paper entitled Le Souvenir du present et la fausse reconnaissance in L'Energie spirituelle, pp. 117-161 (Mind-Energy), Bergson considers cases of an abnormal or fictitious memory, coinciding with perception in rather a strange manner. This does not, however, affect the validity of the above definition.] Bergson first of all draws attention to a distinction between two different forms of Memory, the nature of which will be best brought out by considering two examples. We are fond of giving to children or young persons at school selections from the plays of Shakespeare, "to be learned by heart," as we say. We praise the boy or girl who can repeat a long passage perfectly, and we regard that scholar as gifted with a good memory. To illustrate the second type of case, suppose a question to be put to that boy asking him what he saw on the last half-holiday when he took a ramble in the country. He may, or may not, be able to tell us much of his adventures on that occasion, for whatever he can recall is due to a mental operation of a different character from that which enabled him to learn his lesson. There is here no question of learning by rote, of memorizing, but of capacity to recall to mind a past experience. The boy who is clever at memorizing a passage from Shakespeare may not have a good memory at all for recalling past events. To understand why this is so we must examine these two forms of Memory more closely and refer to Bergson's own words: "I study a lesson, and in order to learn it by heart I read it a first time, accentuating every line; I then repeat it a certain number of times. At each repetition there is progress; the words are more and more linked together, and at last make a continuous whole. When that moment comes, it is said that I know my lesson by heart, that it is imprinted on my memory. I consider now how the lesson has been learnt and picture to myself the successive phases of the process. Each several reading then recurs to me with its own individuality. It is distinguished from those which preceded or followed it, by the place which it occupied in time; in short, each reading stands out before my mind as a definite event in my history. Again it will be said that these images are recollections, that they are imprinted on my Memory. The same words then are used in both cases. Do they mean the same thing? The memory of the lesson which is remembered, in the sense of learned by heart, has ALL the marks of a habit. Like a habit, it is acquired by the repetition of the same effort. Like every habitual bodily exercise, it is stored up in a mechanism which is set in motion as a whole by an initial impulse, in a closed system of automatic movements, which succeed each other in the same order and together take the same length of time. The memory of each several reading, on the contrary, has NONE of the marks of a habit, it is like an event in my life; it is a case of spontaneous recollection as distinct from mere learnt recollection. Now a learnt recollection passes out of time in the measure that the lesson is better known; it becomes more and more impersonal, more and more foreign to our past life." [Footnote: Matter and Memory, pp. 89-90 (Fr. pp. 75-76).] This quotation makes clear that of these two forms of Memory, it is the power of spontaneous recollection which is Memory par excellence and constitutes "real" Memory. The other, to which psychologists usually have devoted most of their attention in discussing the problem of Memory, is habit interpreted as Memory, rather than Memory itself. Having thus made clear this valuable and fundamental distinction — "one of the best things in Bergson" [Footnote: Bertrand Russell's remark in his Philosophy of Bergson, p. 7.]—and having shown that in practical life the automatic memory necessarily plays an important part, often inhibiting "pure" Memory, Bergson proceeds to examine and criticize certain views of Memory itself, and endeavours finally to demonstrate to us what he himself considers it to be.

He takes up the cudgels to attack the view which aims at blending Memory with Perception, as being of like kind. Memory, he argues, must be distinguished from Perception, however much we admit (and rightly) that memories enter into and colour all our perceptions. They are quite different in their nature. A remembrance is the representation of an absent object. We distinguish between hearing a faint tap at the door, and the faint memory of a loud one. We cannot admit the validity of the statement that there is only a difference of intensity between Perception and Recollection. "As our perception of a present object is something of that object itself, our representation of the absent object, as in Memory, must be a phenomenon of quite other order than Perception, since between presence and absence there are no degrees, no intermediate stages." [Footnote: Matter and Memory, p. 315 (Fr. p. 264).] If we maintain that recollection is merely a weakened form of Perception we must note the consequences of such a thesis. "If recollection is only a weakened Perception, inversely, Perception must be something like an intenser Memory. Now, the germ of English Idealism is to be found here. This Idealism consists in finding only a difference of degree and not of kind, between the reality of the object perceived, and the ideality of the object conceived." [Footnote: Matter and Memory, p. 318 (Fr. p. 267).] The maintenance of such a doctrine involves the further remarkable contention that "we construct matter from our own interior states and that perception is only a true hallucination." [Footnote: Matter and Memory, p 318 (Fr. p. 267).] Such a theory will not harmonize with the experienced difference between Perceptions and Memories.[Footnote: Le Souvenir du present et la fausse reconnaissance, Revue philosophique, Dec., 1908, p. 568; also L'Energie spirituelle (Mind-Energy).] We do not mistake the perception of a slight sound for the recollection of a loud noise, as has already been remarked. The consciousness of a recollection "never occurs as a weak state which we try to relegate to the past so soon as we become aware of its weakness. How indeed, unless we already possess the representation of a past, previously lived, could we relegate to it the less intense psychical states, when it would be so simple to set them alongside of strong states as a present experience more confused, beside a present experience more distinct?" [Footnote: Matter and Memory, p. 319 (Fr. p. 268).] The truth is that Memory does not consist in a regression from the present into the past, but on the contrary, in a progress from the past to the present. Memory is radically distinct from Perception, in its character.

Bergson then passes on to discuss other views of Memory, and in particular, those which deal with the nature of Memory and its relation to the brain. It is stated dogmatically by some that Memory is a function of the brain. Others claim, in opposition to this, that Memory is something other than a function of the brain. Between two such statements as these, compromise or reconciliation is obviously impossible. It is then for experience to decide between these two conflicting views. This empirical appeal Bergson does not shirk. He has made a most comprehensive and intensive study of pathological phenomena relating to the mental malady known as aphasia. This particular type of disorder belongs to a whole class of mental diseases known as amnesia. Now amnesia (in Greek, "forgetfulness") is literally any loss or defect of the Memory. Aphasia (in Greek "absence of speech") is a total or partial loss of the power of speech, either in its spoken or written form. The term covers the loss of the power of expression by spoken words, but is often extended to include both word-deafness, i.e., the misunderstanding of what is said, and word-blindness — the inability to read words. An inability to execute the movements necessary to express oneself, either by gesture, writing, or speech, is styled "motor aphasia," to distinguish it from the inability to understand familiar gestures and written or spoken words, which is known as "sensory-aphasia." The commonest causes of this disease are lesions, affecting the special nerve centres, due to haemorrhage or the development of tumours, being in the one case rapid, in the other a gradual development. Of course any severe excitement, fright or illness, involving a disturbance of the normal circulation in the cerebral centres, may produce asphasia. During the war, it has been one of the afflictions of a large number of the victims of "shell-shock." But, whatever be the cause, the patient is reduced mentally to an elementary state, resembling that of a child, and needs re-educating in the elements of language.

Now, from his careful study of the pathological phenomena, manifested in these cases, Bergson draws some very important conclusions in regard to the nature of Memory and its relation to the brain. In 1896, when he brought out his work Matiere et Memoire, in Paris, the general view was against his conclusions and his opinions were ridiculed. By 1910, a marked change had come about and he was able to refer to this in the new introduction. [Footnote: See Bibliography, p. 158.] His view was no longer considered paradoxical. The conception of aphasia, once classical, universally admitted, believed to be unshakeable, had been considerably shaken in that period of fourteen years. Localization, and reference to centres would not, it was found, explain things sufficiently.[Footnote: The work of Pierre Janet was largely influential also in bringing about this change of view.] This involved a too rigid and mechanical conception of the brain as a mere "box," and Bergson attacks it very forcibly under the name of "the box theory." "All the arguments," he says, "from fact which may be invoked in favour of a probable accumulation of memories in the cortical substance, are drawn from local disorders of memory. But if recollections were really deposited in the brain, to definite gaps in memory characteristic lesions of the brain would correspond. Now in those forms of amnesia in which a whole period of our past existence, for example, is abruptly and entirely obliterated from memory, we do not observe any precise cerebral lesion; and on the contrary, in those disorders of memory where cerebral localization is distinct and certain, that is to say, in the different types of aphasia, and in the diseases of visual or auditory recognition, we do not find that certain definite recollections are, as it were, torn from their seat, but that it is the whole faculty of remembering that is more or less diminished in vitality, as if the subject had more or less difficulty in bringing his recollections into contact with the present situation." [Footnote: Matter and Memory, p. 315 (Fr. pp. 264-265).] But as it is a fact that the past survives under two distinct forms, viz., "motor mechanisms" and "independent recollections," we find that this explains why "in all cases where a lesion of the brain attacks a certain category of recollections, the affected recollections do not resemble each other by all belonging to the same period, or by any logical relationship to one another, but simply in that they are all auditive or all visual or all motor. That which is damaged appears to be the various sensorial or motor areas, or more often still, those appendages which permit of their being set going from within the cortex rather than the recollections themselves." [Footnote: Matter and Memory, p. 317 (Fr. p. 266).] Going even further than this, by the study of the recognition of words, and of sensory-aphasia, Bergson shows that "recognition is in no way affected by a mechanical awakening of memories that are asleep in the brain. It implies, on the contrary, a more or less high degree of tension in consciousness, which goes to fetch pure recollections in pure memory, in order to materialize them progressively, by contact with the present perception." [Footnote: Matter and Memory, p. 317 (Fr. p. 266).]

In the face of all this mass of evidence and thoroughness of argument which Bergson brings forward, we are led to conclude that Memory is indeed something other than a function of the brain. Criticizing Wundt's view,[Footnote: As expressed in his Grundzuge der physiologische psychologie, vol. I., pp. 320-327. See Matter and Memory, p. 164 (Fr. p. 137).] Bergson contends that no trace of an image can remain in the substance of the brain and no centre of apperception can exist. "There is not in the brain a region in which memories congeal and accumulate. The alleged destruction of memories by an injury to the brain is but a break in the continuous progress by which they actualize themselves." [Footnote: Matter and Memory, p. 160 (Fr. p. 134).] It is then futile to ask in what spot past memories are stored. To look for them in any place would be as meaningless as asking to see traces of the telephonic message upon the telephone wire.

"Memory," it has been said, "is a faculty which loses nothing and records everything." [Footnote: Ball, quoted by Rouillard, Les Amnesies, Paris, 1885, p. 25; Matter and Memory, p. 201 (Fr. p. 168).] This is only too true, although normally we do not recognize it. But we can never be sure that we have absolutely forgotten anything. Illness, producing delirium, may provoke us to speak of things we had thought were gone beyond recall and which perhaps we even wish were beyond recall. A somnambulistic state or even a dream may show us memory extending far further back than we could ordinarily imagine. The facing of death in battle, we know, recalls to many, with extreme vividness, scenes of early childhood which they had deemed long since forgotten. "There is nothing," says Bergson, "more instructive in this regard than what happens in cases of sudden suffocation — in men drowned or hanged. The man, when brought to life again, states that he saw in a very short time all the forgotten events of his life, passing before him with great rapidity, with their smallest circumstances, and in the very order in which they occurred." [Footnote: La Perception du Changement, pp. 30-31, and Matter and Memory, p 200 (Fr p 168).] Hence we can never be absolutely sure that we have forgotten anything although at any given time we may be unable to recall it to mind. There is an unconscious memory.[Footnote: Cf. Samuel Butler's Unconscious Memory.] Speaking of the profound and yet undeniable reality of the unconscious, Bergson says,[Footnote: Matter and Memory, pp 181-182 (Fr. pp. 152-153). See also Le Souvenir du present et la fausse reconnaissance, Revue philosophique, Dec., 1908, p. 592, and L'Energie spirituelle, pp. 159-161 (Mind-Energy).] "Our unwillingness to conceive unconscious psychical states, is due, above all, to the fact that we hold consciousness to be the essential property of psychical states, so that a psychical state cannot, it seems, cease to be conscious without ceasing to exist. But if consciousness is but the characteristic note of the present, that is to say, of the actually lived, in short, of the active, then that which does not act may cease to belong to consciousness without therefore ceasing to exist in some manner. In other words, in the psychological domain, consciousness may not be the synonym of existence, but only of real action or of immediate efficacy; limiting thus the meaning of the term, we shall have less difficulty in representing to ourselves a psychical state which is unconscious, that is to say, ineffective. Whatever idea we may frame of consciousness in itself, such as it would be if it could work untrammelled, we cannot deny that in a being which has bodily functions, the chief office of consciousness is to preside over action and to enlighten choice. Therefore it throws light on the immediate antecedents of the decision and on those past recollections which can usefully combine with it; all else remains in shadow." But we have no more right to say that the past effaces itself as soon as perceived than to suppose that material objects cease to exist when we cease to perceive them. Memory, to use a geometrical illustration which Bergson himself employs, comes into action like the point of a cone pressing against a plane. The plane denotes the present need, particularly in relation to bodily action, while the cone stands for all our total past. Much of this past, indeed most of it, only endures as unconscious Memory, but it is always capable of coming to the apex of the cone, i.e., coming into consciousness. So we may say that there are different planes of Memory, conic sections, if we keep up the original metaphor, and the largest of these contains all our past. This may be well described as "the plane of dream." [Footnote: See Matter and Memory, p. 222 (Fr. p. 186) and the paper L'Effort intellectuel, Revue philosophique, Jan., 1902, pp. 2 and 25, L'Energie spirituelle, pp. 165 and 199 (Mind-Energy).]

This connexion of Memory with dreams is more fully brought out by Bergson in his lecture before the Institut psychologique international, five years after the publication of Matiere et Memoire, entitled Le Reve. [Footnote: Delivered March 26, 1901. See Bibliography, p. 153.] The following is a brief summary of the view there set forth. Memories, and only memories, weave the web of our dreams. They are "such stuff as dreams are made on." Often we do not recognize them. They may be very old memories, forgotten during waking hours, drawn from the most obscure depths of our past, or memories of objects we have perceived distractedly, almost unconsciously, while awake. They may be fragments of broken memories, composing an incoherent and unrecognizable whole. In a waking state our memories are closely connected with our present situation (unless we be given to day-dreams!). In an animal memory serves to recall to him the advantageous or injurious consequences which have formerly arisen in a like situation, and so aids his present action. In man, memory forms a solid whole, a pyramid whose point is inserted precisely into our present action. But behind the memories which are involved in our occupations, there are others, thousands of others, stored below the scene illuminated by consciousness. "Yes, I believe indeed," says Bergson, "that all our past life is there, preserved even to the most infinitesimal details, and that we forget nothing and that all that we have ever felt, perceived, thought, willed, from the first awakening of our consciousness, survives indestructibly." [Footnote: Dreams, p. 37. For this discussion in full, see pages 34-39, or see L'Energie spirituelle, pp. 100-103 (Mind-Energy).] Of course, in action I have something else to do than occupy myself with these. But suppose I become disinterested in present action — that I fall asleep — then the obstacle (my attention to action) removed, these memories try to raise the trap-door — they all want to get through. From the multitude which are called, which will be chosen? When I was awake, only those were admitted which bore on the present situation. Now, in sleep, more vague images occupy my vision, more indecisive sounds reach my ear, more indistinct touches come to my body, and more vague sensations come from my internal organs. Hence those memories which can assimilate themselves to some element in this vague mass of very indistinct sensations manage to get through. When such union is effected, between memory and sensation, we have a dream.

In order that a recollection should be brought to mind, it is necessary that it should descend from the height of pure memory to the precise point where action is taking place. Such a power is the mark of the well-balanced mind, pursuing a via media between impulsiveness on the one hand, and dreaminess on the other. "The characteristic of the man of action," says Bergson in this connexion, "is the promptitude with which he summons to the help of a given situation all the memories which have reference to it. To live only in the present, to respond to a stimulus by the immediate reaction which prolongs it, is the mark of the lower animals; the man who proceeds in this way is a man of impulse. But he who lives in the past, for the mere pleasure of living there, and in whom recollections emerge into the light of consciousness, without any advantage for the present situation, is hardly better fitted for action; here we have no man of impulse, but a dreamer. Between these two extremes lies the happy disposition of a memory docile enough to follow with precision all the outlines of the present situation, but energetic enough to resist all other appeal. Good sense or practical sense, is probably nothing but this." [Footnote: Matter and Memory, p. 198 (Fr. pp. 166-167).]

In the paper L'Effort intellectuel, contributed in 1902 to the Revue philosophique, and now reprinted in L'Energie spirituelle,[Footnote: Pp. 163-202. See also Mind-Energy.]Bergson gives an analysis of what is involved in intellectual effort. There is at first, he shows, something conceived quite generally, an idea vague and abstract, a schema which has to be completed by distinct images. In thought there is a movement of the mind from the plane of the schema to the plane of the concrete image. Various images endeavour to fit themselves into the schema, or the schema may adapt itself to the reception of the images. These double efforts to secure adaptation and cooperation may both encounter resistance from the other, a situation which is known to us as hesitation, accompanied by the awareness of obstacles, thus involving intellectual effort.

Memory then, Bergson wishes us to realize, in response to his treatment of it, is no mere function of the brain; it is something infinitely more subtle, infinitely more elusive, and more wondrous. Our memories are not stored in the brain like letters in a filing cabinet, and all our past survives indestructibly as Memory, even though in the form of unconscious memory. We must recognize Memory to be a spiritual fact and so regard it as a pivot on which turn many discussions of vital importance when we come to investigate the problem of the relation of soul and body. For "Memory must be, in principle, a power absolutely independent of matter. If then, spirit is a reality, it is here, in the phenomenon of Memory that we may come into touch with it experimentally." [Footnote: Matter and Memory, p. 81 (Fr. p. 68).] "Memory," he would remind us finally, "is just the intersection of mind and matter." [Footnote: Matter and Memory, Introduction, p. xii.] "A remembrance cannot be the result of a state of the brain. The state of the brain continues the remembrance; it gives it a hold on the present by the materiality which it confers upon it, but pure memory is a spiritual manifestation. With Memory, we are, in very truth, in the domain of spirit." [Footnote: Matter and Memory, p. 320 (Fr. p. 268).]

CHAPTER V
THE RELATION OF SOUL AND BODY

The hypothesis of Psycho-physical Parallelism — Not to be accepted uncritically — Bergson opposes it, and shows the hypothesis to rest on a confusion of terms. Bergson against Epiphenomenalism — Soul-life unique and wider than the brain — Telepathy, subconscious action and psychical research — Souls and survival.

For philosophy in general, and for psychology in particular, the problem of the relation of soul and body has prime significance, and moreover, it is a problem with which each of us is acquainted intimately and practically, even if we know little or nothing of the academic discussions, or of the technical terms representing various views. It is very frequently the terminology which turns the plain man away from the consideration of philosophical problems; but he has some conception, however crude it may be, of his soul or his mind and of his body. These terms are familiar to him, but the sight of a phrase like "psycho-physical parallelism" rather daunts him. Really, it stands for quite a simple thing, and is just the official label used to designate the theory commonly held by scientific men of all kinds, to describe the relation of soul and body. Put more precisely, it is just the assertion that brain and consciousness work on parallel lines.

Bergson does not accept the hypothesis of psycho-physical parallelism. In the first of his four lectures on La Nature de l'Ame, given at London University in 1911, we find him criticizing the notion that consciousness has no independence of its own, that it merely expresses certain states of the brain, that the content of a fact of consciousness is to be found wholly in the corresponding cerebral state. It is true that we should not find many physiologists or philosophers who would tell us now that "the brain secretes thought as the liver secretes bile." [Footnote: Cabanis (1757-1808). Rapports du physique et du morale de l'homme, 1802. See quotation by William James in Human Immortality. Note (4) in his Appendix.] But there was an idea that, if we could see through the skull and observe what takes place in the brain, if we had an enormously powerful microscope which would permit us to follow the movements of the molecules, atoms, electrons, of the brain, and if we had the key to the correspondence between these phenomena and the mind, we should know all the thoughts and wishes of the person to whom the brain belonged—we should see what took place in his soul, as a telegraph operator could read by the oscillation of his needles the meaning of a message which was sent through his instrument. The notion of an equality or parallelism between conscious activity and cerebral activity, was commonly adopted by modern physiology, and it was adopted without discussion as a scientific notion by the majority of philosophers. Yet the experimental basis of this theory is extremely slight, indeed altogether insufficient, and in reality the theory is a metaphysical conception, resulting from the views of the seventeenth century thinkers who had hopes of "a universal mathematic." The idea had been accepted that all was capable of determination in the psychical as well as the physical world, inasmuch as the psychical was only a reflex of the physical. Parallelism was adopted by science because of its convenience.[Footnote: See The Times of Oct. 21, 1911.] Bergson, however, pointed out that philosophy ought not to accept it without criticism, and maintained, moreover, that it could not stand the criticism that might be brought against it. Relation of soul and body was undeniable, but that it was a parallel or equivalent relation he denied most emphatically. That criticism he had launched himself with great vigour in 1901 at a Meeting of the Societe francaise de philosophie,[Footnote: See Bibliography, p. 153.] and on a more memorable occasion, at the International Congress of Philosophy at Geneva in 1904.[Footnote: See Bibliography, p. 154.] Before the Philosophical Society he lectured on Le Parallelisme psycho-physique et la Metaphysique positive, and propounded the following propositions:

1. If psycho-physical parallelism is neither rigorous nor complete, if to every determined thought there does not correspond an absolutely determined state (si a toute pensee determinee ne correspond pas un etat cerebral determine absolument), it will be the business of experience to mark with increasing accuracy the precise points at which parallelism begins and ends.

2. If this empirical inquiry is possible, it will measure more and more exactly the separation between the thought and the physical conditions in which this thought is exercised. In other words, it will give us a progressive knowledge of the relation of man as a thinking being to man as a living being, and therefore of what may be termed "the meaning of Life."

3. If this meaning of Life can be empirically determined more and more exactly, and completely, a positive metaphysic is possible: that is to say, a metaphysic which cannot be contested and which will admit of a direct and indefinite progress; such a metaphysic would escape the objections urged against a transcendental metaphysic, and would be strictly scientific in form.

After having propounded these propositions, he defended them by recalling much of the data considered in his work Matiere et Memoire which he had published five years previously and which has been examined in the previous chapter. The onus of proof lay, said Bergson, with the upholders of parallelism. It is a purely metaphysical hypothesis unwarrantable in his opinion as a dogma. He distinguishes between correspondence — which he of course admits — and parallelism, to which he is opposed. We never think without a certain substratum of cerebral activity, but what the relation is precisely, between brain and consciousness, is one for long and patient research: it cannot be determined a priori and asserted dogmatically. Until such investigation has been carried out, it behoves us to be undogmatic and not to allege more than the facts absolutely warrant, that is to say, a relation of correspondence. Parallelism is far too simple an explanation to be a true one. Before the International Congress, Bergson launched another attack on parallelism which caused quite a little sensation among those present. Says M. E. Chartier, in his report: La lecture de ce memoire, lecture qui commandait l'attention a provoque chez presque tous les auditeurs un mouvement de surprise et d'inquietude. [Footnote: The paper Le Paralogisme psycho-physiologique is given in Revue de metaphysique et de morale, Nov., 1904, pp. 895-908. The Discussion in the Congress is given on pp. 1027-1037. This was reissued under the title Le Cerveau et la Pensee: une illusion philosophique in the collected volume of essays and lectures, published in 1919, L'Energie spirituelle, pp. 203-223 (Mind-Energy).] He there set out to show that Parallelism cannot be consistently stated from any point of view, for it rests on a fallacious argument — on a fundamental contradiction. To grasp Bergson's points in this argument, the reading of this paper in the original, as a whole, is necessary. It is difficult to condense it and keep its clearness of thought. Briefly, it amounts to this, that the formulation of the doctrine of Parallelism rests on an ambiguity in the terms employed in its statement, that it contains a subtle dialectical artifice by which we pass surreptitiously from one system of notation to another ignoring the substitution: logically, we ought to keep to one system of notation throughout. The two systems are: Idealism and Realism. Bergson attempts to show that neither of these separately can admit Parallelism, and that Parallelism cannot be formulated except by a confusion of the two — by a process of mental see-sawing as it were, which of course we are not entitled to perform, Idealism and Realism being two opposed and contradictory views of reality. For the Idealist, things external to the mind are images, and of these the brain is one. Yet the images are in the brain. This amounts to saying that the whole is contained in the part. We tend, however, to avoid this by passing to a pseudo-realistic position by saying that the brain is a thing and not an image. This is passing over to the other system of notation. For the Realist it is the essence of reality to suppose that there are things behind representations. Some Realists maintain that the brain actually creates the representation, which is the doctrine of Epiphenomenalism: while others hold the view of the Occasionalists, and others posit one reality underlying both. All however agree in upholding Parallelism. In the hands of the Realist, the theory is equivalent to asserting that a relation between two terms is equal to one of them. This involves contradiction and Realism then crosses over to the other system of notation. It cannot do without Idealism: science itself oscillates from the one system to the other. We cannot admit Parallelism as a dogma—as a metaphysical truth—however useful it may be as a working hypothesis.

Bergson then proceeds to state and to criticize some of the mischievous ideas which arise from Parallelism. There is the idea of a brain-soul, of a spot where the soul lives or where the brain thinks—which we have not quite abandoned since Descartes named the pineal gland as the seat of the soul. Then there is the false idea that all causality is mechanistic and that there is nothing in the universe which is not mathematically calculable. There is the confusion of representations and of things. There is the false notion that we may argue that if two wholes are bound together there must be an equivalent relation of the parts. Bergson points out in this connexion that the absence or the presence of a screw can stop a machine or keep it going, but the parts of the screw do not correspond to the parts of the machine. In his new introduction to Matiere et Memoire, he said, "There is a close connexion between a state of consciousness and the brain: this we do not dispute. But there is also a close connexion between a coat and the nail on which it hangs, for if the nail is pulled out the coat falls to the ground. Shall we say then that the shape of the nail gives us the shape of the coat or in any way corresponds to it? No more are we entitled to conclude because the psychical fact is hung on to a cerebral state that there is any parallelism between the two series psychical and physiological." [Footnote: There must be an awkward misprint "physical" for "psychical" in the English translation, p. xi.] Our observation and experience, and science itself, strictly speaking, do not allow us to assert more than that there exists a certain CORRESPONDENCE between brain and consciousness. The psychical and the physical are inter-dependent but not parallel.

Bergson however has more to assert than merely the inadequacy and falsity of Parallelism or Epiphenomenalism. This last theory merely adds consciousness to physical facts as a kind of phosphorescent gleam, resembling, in Bergson's words, a "streak of light following the movement of a match rubbed along a wall in the dark." [Footnote: L'Ame et le Corps, pp. 12-13, in Le Materialisme actuel, or pp. 35-36 of L'Energie spirituelle

(Mind-Energy).] He maintains, as against all this, the irreducibility of the mental, our utter inability to interpret consciousness in terms of anything else, the life of the soul being unique. He further claims that this psychical life is wider and richer than we commonly suppose. The brain is the organ of attention to life. What was said in regard to memory and the brain is applicable to all our mental life. The mind or soul is wider than the brain in every direction, and the brain's activity corresponds to no more than an infinitesimal part of the activity of the mind. [Footnote: L'Ame et le Corps, Le Materialisme actuel, p. 45, L'Energie spirituelle, p. 61.] This is expressed more clearly in his Presidential Address to the British Society for Psychical Research at the Aeolian Hall, London, 1913, where he remarked, "The cerebral life is to the mental life what the movements of the baton of a conductor are to the symphony." [Footnote: The Times, May 29, 1913.] Such a remark contains fruitful suggestions to all engaged in Psychical Research, and to all persons interested in the fascinating study of telepathy. Bergson is of the opinion that we are far less definitely cut off from each other, soul from soul, than we are body from body. "It is space," he says, "which creates multiplicity and distinction. It is by their bodies that the different human personalities are radically distinct. But if it is demonstrated that human consciousness is partially independent of the human brain, since the cerebral life represents only a small part of the mental life, it is very possible that the separation between the various human consciousnesses or souls, may not be so radical as it seems to be." [Footnote: The Times, May 29, 1913.] There may be, he suggests, in the psychical world, a process analogous to what is known in the physical world as "endosmosis." Pleading for an impartial and frank investigation of telepathy, he pointed out that it was probable, or at least possible, that it was taking place constantly as a subtle and sub-conscious influence of soul on soul, but too feebly to be noticed by active consciousness, or it was neutralized by certain obstacles. We have no right to deny its possibility on the plea of its being supernatural, or against natural law, for our ignorance does not entitle us to say what may be natural or not. If telepathy does not square at all well with our preconceived notions, it may be more true that our preconceived notions are false than that telepathy is fictitious; especially will this be so if our notion of the relation of soul and body be based on Parallelism. We must overcome this prejudice and seek to make others set it aside. Telepathy and the sub-conscious mental life combine to make us realize the wonder of the soul. It is not spatial, it is spiritual. Bergson insists strongly on the unity of our conscious life. Merely associationist theories are vicious in this respect: they try to resolve the whole into parts, and then neglect the whole in their concentration on the parts. All psychological investigation incurs this risk of dealing with abstractions. "Psychology, in fact, proceeds like all the other sciences by analysis. It resolves the self which has been given to it at first in a simple intuition, into sensations, feelings, ideas, etc., which it studies separately. It substitutes then for the self a series of elements which form the facts of psychology. But are these elements really parts? That is the whole question, and it is because it has been evaded that the problem of human personality has so often been stated in insoluble terms." [Footnote: Introduction to Metaphysics, p. 21.] "Personality cannot be composed of psychical states even if there be added to them a kind of thread for the purpose of joining the states together." [Footnote: Introduction to Metaphysics, p. 25.] We shall never make the soul fit into a category or succeed in applying concepts to our inner life. The life of the soul is wider than the brain and wider than all intellectual constructions or moulds we may attempt to form. It is a creative force capable of producing novelty in the world: it creates actions and can, in addition, create itself.

Philosophy shows us "the life of the body just where it really is, on the road that leads to the life of the spirit"; our powers of sense impression and of intelligence are both instruments in the service of the will. With a little will one can do much if one places the will in the right direction. For this force of will which is the essence of the soul or personality has these exceptional characteristics, that its intensity depends on its direction, and that its quality may become the creator of quantity. [Footnote: See the lectures La Nature de l'Ame.] The brain and the body in general are instruments of the soul. The brain orients the mind toward action, it is the point of attachment between the spirit and its material environment. It is like the point of a knife to the blade — it enables it to penetrate into the realm of action or, to give another of Bergson's metaphors, it is like the prow of the ship, enabling the soul to penetrate the billows of reality. Yet, for all that, it limits and confines the life of the spirit; it narrows vision as do the blinkers which we put on horses. We must, however, abandon the notion of any rigid and determined parallelism between soul and body and accustom ourselves to the fact that the life of the mind is wider than the limits of cerebral activity. And further, there is this to consider — "The more we become accustomed to this idea of a consciousness which overflows the organ we call the brain, then the more natural and probable we find the hypothesis that the soul survives the body. For were the mental exactly modelled on the cerebral, we might have to admit that consciousness must share the fate of the body and die with it." [Footnote: New York Times, Sept. 27, 1914.] "But the destiny of consciousness is not bound up with the destiny of cerebral matter." [Footnote: Creative Evolution, p. 285 (Fr. p. 293).] "Although the data is not yet sufficient to warrant more than an affirmation of high probability," [Footnote: Louis Levine's interview with Bergson, New York Times, Feb. 22, 1914. Quoted by Miller, Bergson and Religion, p. 268.] yet it leaves the way open for a belief in a future life and creates a presumption in favour of a faith in immortality. "Humanity," as Bergson remarks, "may, in its evolution, overcome the most formidable of its obstacles, perhaps even death." [Footnote: Creative Evolution, p. 286 (Fr. p. 294). In Life and Consciousness he says we may admit that in man at any rate "Consciousness pursues its path beyond this earthly life" Cf. also conclusion to La Conscience el la Vie in L'Energie spirituelle, p. 29, and to L'Ame et le Corps, in the same vol., p. 63.]

The great error of the spiritual philosophers has been the idea that by isolating the spiritual life from all the rest, by suspending it in space, as high as possible above the earth, they were placing it beyond attack; as if they were not, thereby, simply exposing it to be taken as an effect of mirage! Certainly they are right to believe in the absolute reality of the person and in his independence of matter: but science is there which shows the inter-dependence of conscious life and cerebral activity. When a strong instinct assures the probability of personal survival, they are right not to close their ears to its voice; but if there exist "souls" capable of an independent life, whence do they come? When, how, and why do they enter into this body which we see arise quite naturally from a mixed cell derived from the bodies of its two parents? [Footnote: Creative Evolution, p. 283 (Fr. p. 291).] At the close of the Lectures on La Nature de l'Ame, Bergson suggests, by referring to an allegory of Plotinus, in regard to the origin of souls, that in the beginning there was a general interpenetration of souls which was equivalent to the very principle of life, and that the history of the evolution of life on this planet shows this principle striving until man's consciousness has been developed, and thus personalities have been able to constitute themselves. "Souls are being created which, in a sense, pre-existed. They are nothing else but the little rills into which the great river of life divides itself, flowing through the great body of humanity." [Footnote: Creative Evolution, p. 284 (Fr. p. 292).]

CHAPTER VI
TIME—TRUE AND FALSE

Our ordinary conception of Time false because it is spatial and homogeneous—Real Time (la duree) not spatial or homogeneous—Flow of consciousness a qualitative multiplicity—The real self and the external self. La duree and the life of the self—No repetition—Personality and the accumulation of experience-Change and la duree as vital elements in the universe.

For any proper understanding of Bergson's thought, it is necessary to grasp his views regarding Time, for they are fundamental factors in his philosophy and serve to distinguish it specially from that of previous thinkers. It is interesting to note however, in passing, that Dr. Ward, in his Realm of Ends, claims to have anticipated Bergson's view of Concrete Time. In discussing the relation of such Time to the conception of God, he says, "I think I may fairly claim to have anticipated him (Bergson) to some extent. In 1886 I had written a long paragraph on this topic." [Footnote: See The Realm of Ends' foot-note on pp. 306-7. Ward is referring to his famous article in the Encyclopaedia Britannica, eleventh edition, Psychology, p. 577 (now revised and issued in book form as Psychological Principles).] Be this as it may, no philosopher has made so much of this view of Time as Bergson. One might say it is the corner-stone of his philosophy, for practically the whole of it is built upon his conception of Time. His first large work, Essai sur les donnees immediates de la conscience, or, to give it its better title, in English, Time and Free Will, appeared in 1889.

Our ordinary conception of Time, that which comes to us from the physical sciences, is, Bergson maintains, a false one. It is false because so far from being temporal in character, it is spatial. We look upon space as a homogeneous medium without boundaries; yet we look on Time too, as just such another medium, homogeneous and unlimited. Now here is an obvious difficulty, for since homogeneity consists in being without qualities, it is difficult to see how one homogeneity can be distinguished from another. This difficulty is usually avoided by the assertion that homogeneity takes two forms, one in which its contents co-exist, and another in which they follow one another. Space, then, we say, is that homogeneous medium in which we are aware of side-by-sideness, Time — that homogeneous medium in which we are aware of an element of succession. But this surely we are not entitled to maintain, for we are then distinguishing two supposed homogeneities by asserting a difference of quality in them. To do so is to take away homogeneity. We must think again and seek a way out of this difficulty. Let us admit space to be a homogeneous medium without bounds. Then every homogeneous medium without bounds must be space. What, then, becomes of Time? — for on this showing, Time becomes space. Yes, says Bergson, that is so, for our common view of Time is a false one, being really a hybrid conception, a spurious concept due to the illicit introduction of the idea of space, and to our application of the notion of space, which is applicable to physical objects, to states of consciousness, to which it is really inapplicable. Objects occupying space are marked out as external to one another, but this cannot be said of conscious states. Yet, in our ordinary speech and conventional view of things, we think of conscious states as separated from one another and as spread out like "things," in a fictitious, homogeneous medium to which we give the name Time. Bergson says, "At any rate, we cannot finally admit two forms of the homogeneous, Time and Space, without first seeking whether one of them cannot be reduced to the other. Now, externality is the distinguishing mark of things which occupy space, while states of consciousness are not essentially external to one another and become so only by being spread out in Time regarded as a homogeneous medium. If, then, one of these two supposed forms of the homogeneous, viz., Time and Space, is derived from the other, we can surmise a priori that the idea of space is the fundamental datum. Time, conceived under the form of an unbounded and homogeneous medium, is nothing but the ghost of space, haunting the reflective consciousness." [Footnote: Time and Free Will, p. 98 (Fr. p. 75).] Bergson remarks that Kant's great mistake was to take Time as a homogeneous medium. [Footnote: Time and Free Will, p. 232 (Fr. p. 178).]

Having asserted the falsity of the view of Time ordinarily held, Bergson proceeds to make clear to us his view of what Real Time is — an undertaking by no means easy for him, endeavouring to lay before us the subtleties of this problem, nor for us who endeavour to interpret his language and grasp his meaning. We are indeed here face to face with what is one of the most difficult sections of his philosophy. An initial difficulty meets us in giving a definite name to the Time which Bergson regards as so real, as opposed to the spatial falsity, masquerading as Time, whose true colours he has revealed. In the original French text Bergson employs the term duree to convey his meaning. But for the translation of this into English there is no term which will suffice and which will adequately convey to the reader, without further exposition, the wealth of meaning intended to be conveyed. "Duration" is usually employed by translators as the nearest approach possible in English. The inadequacy of language is never more keenly felt than in dealing with fundamental problems of thought. Its chief mischief is its all-too-frequent ambiguity. In the following remarks the original French term la duree will be used in preference to the English word "Duration."

The distinction between the false Time and true Time may be regarded as a distinction between mathematical Time and living Time, or between abstract and concrete Time. This living, concrete Time is that true Time of which Bergson endeavours to give us a conception as la duree. He has criticized the abstract mathematical Time, his attack having been made to open up the way for a treatment of what he really considers Time to be. Now, from the arguments previously mentioned, it follows that Time, Real Time, which is radically different from space, cannot be any homogeneous medium. It is heterogeneous in character. We are aware of it in relation to ourselves, for it has reference not to the existence of a multiplicity of material objects in space, but to a multiplicity of a quite different nature, entirely non-spatial, viz., that of conscious states. Being non-spatial, such a multiplicity cannot be composed of elements which are external to one another as are the objects existing in space. States of consciousness are not in any way external to one another. Indeed, they interpenetrate to such a degree that even the use of the word "state" is apt to be misleading. As we saw in the chapter on The Reality of Change, there can be strictly no states of consciousness, for consciousness is not static but dynamic. Language and conventional figures of speech, of which the word "state" itself is a good example, serve to cut up consciousness artificially, but, in reality, it is, as William James termed it, "a stream" and herein lies the essence of Bergson's duree — the Real as opposed to the False Time. "Pure Duration" (la duree pure), he says, "is the form which the succession of our conscious states assumes when our Ego lets itself live, when it refrains from separating its present state from its former states. For this purpose, it need not be entirely absorbed in the passing sensation or idea, for then, on the contrary, it would no longer 'endure.' Nor need it forget its former states; it is enough that in recalling these states, it does not set them alongside its actual state as one point alongside another, but forms both the past and the present states into an organic whole, as happens when we recall the notes of a tune, melting, so to speak, into one another. Might it not be said that even if these notes succeed one another, yet, we perceive them in one another, and that their totality may be compared to a living being whose parts, although distinct, permeate one another just because they are so closely connected?" [Footnote: Time and

Free Will, p. 100 (Fr. p. 76).] Such a duration is Real Time. Unfortunately, we, obsessed by the idea of space, introduce it unwittingly and set our states of consciousness side by side in such a way as to perceive them alongside one another; in a word, we project them into space and we express duree in terms of extensity and succession thus takes the form of a continuous line or a chain—the parts of which touch without interpenetrating one another. [Footnote: Time and Free Will, p. 100 (Fr. p. 76).] Thus is brought to birth that mongrel form, that hybrid conception of False Time criticized above. Real Time, la duree, is not, however, susceptible like False Time to measurement, for it is, strictly speaking, not quantitative in character, but is rather a qualitative multiplicity. "Real Duration (la duree reele) is just what has always been called Time, but it is Time perceived as indivisible." [Footnote: La Perception du Changement, p. 26. Cf. the whole of the Second Lecture.] Certainly pure consciousness does not perceive Time as a sum of units of duration, for, left to itself, it has no means and even no reason to measure Time, but a feeling which lasted only half the number of days, for example, would no longer be the same feeling for it. It is true that when we give this feeling a certain name, when we treat it as a thing, we believe that we can diminish its duration by half, for example, and also halve the duration of all the rest of our history. It seems that it would still be the same life only on a reduced scale. But we forget that states of consciousness are processes and not things; that they are alive and therefore constantly changing, and that, in consequence, it is impossible to cut off a moment from them without making them poorer by the loss of some impression and thus altering their quality. [Footnote: Time and Free Will, p. 196 (Fr. p. 150).] La duree appears as a "wholly qualitative multiplicity, an absolute heterogeneity of elements which pass over into one another." [Footnote: Time and Free Will, p. 229 (Fr. p. 176).] Such a time cannot be measured by clocks or dials but only by conscious beings, for "it is the very stuff of which life and consciousness are made." Intellect does not grasp Real Time—we can only have an intuition of it. "We do not think Real Time—but we live it because life transcends intellect."

In order to bring out the distinctly qualitative character of such a conception of Time, Bergson says, "When we hear a series of blows of a hammer, the sounds form an indivisible melody in so far as they are pure sensations, and here again give rise to a dynamic progress; but, knowing that the same objective cause is at work, we cut up this progress into phases which we then regard as identical; and this multiplicity of elements no longer being conceivable except by being set out in space—since they have now become identical—we are, necessarily, led to the idea of a homogeneous Time, the symbolical image of la duree." [Footnote: Time and Free Will, p. 125 (Fr. pp.

94-95).] "Whilst I am writing these lines," he continues, "the hour strikes on a neighbouring clock, but my inattentive ear does not perceive it until several strokes have made themselves heard. Hence, I have not counted them and yet I only have to turn my attention backwards, to count up the four strokes which have already sounded, and add them to those which I hear. If, then, I question myself carefully on what has just taken place, I perceive that the first four sounds had struck my ear and even affected my consciousness, but that the sensations produced by each one of them, instead of being set side by side, had melted into one another in such a way as to give the whole a peculiar quality, to make a kind of musical phrase out of it. In order, then, to estimate retrospectively, the number of strokes sounded, I tried to reconstruct this phrase in thought; my imagination made one stroke, then two, then three, and as long as it did not reach the exact number, four, my feeling, when consulted, was qualitatively different. It had thus ascertained, in its own way, the succession of four strokes, but quite otherwise than by a process of addition and without bringing in the image of a juxtaposition of distinct terms. In a word, the number of strokes was perceived as a quality and not as a quantity; it is thus that la duree is presented to immediate consciousness and it retains this form so long as it does not give place to a symbolical representation, derived from extensity." [Footnote: Time and Free Will, pp. 127-8 (Fr. pp. 96-97).] In these words Bergson endeavours to drive home his contention that la duree is essentially qualitative. He is well aware of the results of "the breach between quality and quantity," between true duration and pure extensity. He sees its implications in regard to vital problems of the self, of causality and of freedom. Its specific bearing on the problems of freedom and causality we shall discuss in the following chapter. As regards the self, Bergson recognizes that we have much to gain by keeping up the illusion through which we make our conscious states share in the reciprocal externality of outer things, because this distinctness and solidification enables us to give them fixed names in spite of their instability, and distinct names in spite of their interpenetration. Above all it enables us to objectify them, to throw them out into the current of social life. But just for this very reason we are in danger of living our lives superficially and of covering up our real self. We are generally content with what is but a shadow of the real self, projected into space. Consciousness, goaded on by an insatiable desire to separate, substitutes the symbol for the reality or perceives the reality only through the symbol. As the self thus refracted and thereby broken in pieces, is much better adapted to the requirements of social life in general, and of language in particular, consciousness prefers it and gradually loses sight of the fundamental self which is a qualitative multiplicity of conscious states flowing, interpenetrating, melting into one another, and forming an organic whole, a living unity or personality. It is through a consideration of la duree and what it implies that Bergson is led on to the distinction of two selves in each of us.

Towards the close of his essay on Time and Free Will, he points out that there are finally two different selves, a fundamental self and a social self. We reach the former by deep introspection which leads us to grasp our inner states as living things, constantly becoming, never amenable to measure, which permeate one another and of which the succession in la duree has nothing in common with side-by-sideness. But the moments at which we thus grasp ourselves are rare; the greater part of our time we live outside ourselves, hardly perceiving anything of ourselves but our own ghost—a colourless shadow which is but the social representation of the real and largely concealed Ego. Hence our life unfolds in space rather than in time. We live for the external world rather than for ourselves, we speak rather than think, we are "acted" rather than "act" ourselves. To act freely, however, is to recover possession of one's real self and to get back into la duree reele. [Footnote: Time and Free Will, p. 232 (Fr. p. 178).]

Real Time, then, is a living reality, not discrete, not spatial in character—an utter contrast to that fictitious Time with which so many thinkers have busied themselves, setting up "as concrete reality the distinct moments of a Time which they have reduced to powder, while the unity which enables us to call the grains 'powder' they hold to be much more artificial. Others place themselves in the eternal. But as their eternity remains, notwithstanding, abstract since it is empty, being the eternity of a concept which by hypothesis excludes from itself the opposing concept, one does not see how this eternity would permit of an indefinite number of moments co-existing in it, an eternity of death, since it is nothing else than the movement emptied of the mobility which made its life." [Footnote: An Introduction to Metaphysics, pp. 51-54.] The true view of Time, as la duree, would make us see it as a duration which expands, contracts, and intensifies itself more and more; at the limit would be eternity, no longer conceptual eternity, which is an eternity of death, but an eternity of life and change—a living, and therefore still moving, eternity in which our own particular duree would be included as the vibrations are in light, [Footnote: Speaking in Matter and Memory on the Tension of la duree, Bergson calls attention to the "trillions of vibrations" which give rise to our sensation of red light, p. 272 (Fr. p. 229) Cf. La Conscience et la Vie in L'Energie spirituelle, p. 16.] an eternity which would be the concentration of all duree. Altering the old classical phrase sub specie aeternitatis, to suit his special view of Time, Bergson urges us to strive to perceive all things sub specie durationis. [Footnote: La Perception du Changement, p. 36.]

Finally, Bergson reminds us that if our existence were composed of separate states, with an impassive Ego to unite them, for us there would be no duration, for an Ego which does not change, does not endure. La duree, however, is the foundation of our being and is, as we feel, the very substance of the world in which we live. Associating his view of Real Time with the reality of change, he points out that nothing is more resistant or more substantial than la duree, for our duree is not merely one instant replacing another—if it were there would never be anything but the present, no prolonging of the past into the actual, no growth of personality, and no evolution of the universe. La duree is the continuous progress of the past which gnaws into the future and which swells as it advances, leaving on all things its bite, or the mark of its tooth. This being so, consciousness cannot go through the same state twice; history does never really repeat itself. Our personality is being built up each instant with its accumulated experience; it shoots, grows, and ripens without ceasing. We are reminded of George Eliot's lines:

"Our past still travels with us from afar

And what we have been makes us what we are."

For our consciousness this is what we mean by the term "exist." "For a

conscious being, to exist is to change, to change is to mature, and to

go on creating oneself endlessly." [Footnote: Creative Evolution, p.

8 (Fr. p. 8).] Real Time has, then, a very vital meaning for us as

conscious beings, indeed for all that lives, for the organism which

lives is a thing that "endures." "Wherever anything lives," says

Bergson, "there is a register in which Time is being inscribed. This, it

will be said, is only a metaphor. It is of the very essence of mechanism

in fact, to consider as metaphorical every expression which attributes

to Time an effective action and a reality of its own. In vain does

immediate experience show us that the very basis of our conscious

existence is Memory—that is to say, the prolongation of the past into

the present, or in a word, duree, acting and irreversible." [Footnote:

Creative Evolution, p. 17 (Fr. pp. 17-18).] Time is falsely assumed to

have just as much reality for a living being as for an hour-glass. But

if Time does nothing, it is nothing. It is, however, in Bergson's view,

vital to the whole of the universe. He expressly denies that la duree is

merely subjective; the universe "endures" as a whole. In Time and Free

Will it did not seem to matter whether we regarded our inner life as

*having duree or as actually being duree. In the first instance, if we
have duree it is then only an aspect of reality, but if our personality
itself is duree, then Time is reality itself. He develops this last
point of view more explicitly in his later works, and la duree is
identified not only with the reality of change, but with memory and
with*

*spirit. [Footnote: La Perception du Changement, Lecture 2.] In it he
finds the substance of a universe whose reality is change. "God," said
Plato, "being unable to make the world eternal, gave it Time — a moving
image of reality." Bergson himself quotes this remark of Plato, and
seems to have a vision like that of Rosetti's "Blessed Damozel," who
...... "saw*

Time like a pulse shake fierce

Through all the worlds."

The more we study Time, the more we may grasp this vision ourselves,
and then we shall comprehend that la duree implies invention, the creation
of new forms, the continual elaboration of the absolutely new — in short, an
evolution which is creative.

CHAPTER VII
FREEDOM OF THE WILL

Spirit of man revolts from physical and psychological determinism—Former examined and rejected—The latter more subtle—Vice of "associationism"—Psychology without a self. Condemnation of psychological determinism—Room for freedom—The self in action—Astronomical forecasts—Foreseeableness of any human action impossible—Human wills centres of indetermination—Not all our acts free—True freedom, self-determination.

Before passing on to an examination of Bergson's treatment of Evolution, we must consider his discussion of the problem of Freedom of the Will. Few problems which have occupied the attention of philosophers have been more discussed or have given rise to more controversy than that of Freedom. This is, of course, natural as the question at issue is one of very great importance, not merely as speculative, but also in the realm of action. We ask ourselves: "Are we really free?" Can we will either of two or more possibilities which are put before us, or, on the other hand, is everything fixed, predestined in such a way that an all-knowing consciousness could foretell from our past what course our future action would take?

The study of the physical sciences has led to a general acceptance of a principle of causality which is of such a kind that there seems no place in the universe for human freedom. Further, there is a type of psychology which gives rise to the belief that even mental occurrences are as determined as those of the physical world, thus leaving no room for autonomy of the Will. But even when presented with the arguments which make up the case for physical or psychological determinism, the spirit of man revolts from it, refuses to accept it as final, and believes that, in some way or other, the case for Freedom may be maintained. It is at this point that Bergson offers us some help in the solution of the problem, by his Essai sur les donnees immediates de la conscience, better described by its English title Time and Free Will.

The arguments for physical determinism are based on the view that Freedom is incompatible with the fundamental properties of matter, and in particular, with the principle of the conservation of energy. This principle "has been assumed to admit of no exception; there is not an atom either in the nervous system or in the whole of the universe whose position is not determined by the sum of the mechanical actions which the other atoms exert upon it. And the mathematician who knew the position of the molecules or atoms of a human organism at a given moment, as well as the position and motion of all the atoms in the universe, capable of influencing it, could calculate with unfailing certainty the past, present, and future actions of the person to whom this organism belonged, just as one predicts an astronomical phenomenon." [Footnote: Time and Free Will, p. 144 (Fr. p. 110).] Now, it follows that if we admit the universal applicability of such a theory as that of the conservation of energy, we are maintaining that the whole universe is capable of explanation on purely mechanical principles, inherent in the units of which the universe is composed. Hence, the relative position of all units at a given moment, whatever be their nature, strictly determines what their position will be in the succeeding moments, and this mechanistic succession goes on like a Juggernaut car with crushing unrelentlessness, giving rise to a rigid fatalism:

> *"The moving finger writes; and having writ*
>
> *Moves on: nor all thy Piety nor Wit*
>
> *Shall lure it back to cancel half a line,*
>
> *Nor all thy tears wash out a Word of it."*

Is there no way out of this cramping circle? We feel vaguely, intuitively, that there is. Bergson points out to us a way. Even if we admit, he says, that the direction and the velocity of every atom of matter in the universe (including cerebral matter, i.e., the brain, which is a material thing) are strictly determined, it would not at all follow from the acceptance of this theorem that our mental life is subject to the same necessity. For that to be the case, we should have to show absolutely that a strictly determined psychical state corresponds to a definite cerebral state. This, as we have seen, has not been proved. It is admitted that to some psychical states of a limited kind certain cerebral states do correspond, but we have no warrant whatever for concluding that, because the physiological and the psychological series exhibit some corresponding terms, the two series are absolutely parallel. "To extend this parallelism to the series themselves, in their totality, is to settle a priori the problem of freedom." [Footnote: Time and Free Will, p. 147 (Fr. pp. 112-113).] How far the two series do run parallel is a question — as we saw in the chapter on the relation of Soul and Body — for experience, observation, and experiment to decide. The cases which are parallel are limited, and involve facts which are independent of the power of the Will.

Bergson then proceeds to an examination of the more subtle and plausible case for psychological determinism. A very large number of our actions are due to some motive. There you have it, says the psychological determinist. Your so-called Freedom of the Will is a fiction; in reality it is merely the strongest motive which prevails and you imagine that you "freely willed it." But then we must ask him to define "strongest," and here is the fallacy of his argument, for there is no other test of which is the strongest motive, than that it has prevailed. Such statements do not help to solve the difficulty at all, for they avoid it and attempt to conceal it; they are due to a conception of mind which is both false and mischievous, viz., Associationism. This view regards the self as a collection of psychical states. The existing state of consciousness is regarded as necessitated by the preceding states. As, however, even the associationist is aware that these states differ from one another in quality, he cannot attempt to deduce any one of them a priori from its predecessors. He therefore endeavours to find a link connecting the two states. That there is such a link as the simple "association of ideas" Bergson would not think of denying. What he does deny however, very emphatically, is the associationist statement that this relation which explains the transition is the cause of it. Even when admitting a certain truth in the associationist view, it is difficult to maintain that an act is absolutely determined by its motive, and our conscious states by one another. The real mischief of this view lies, however, in the fact, that it misrepresents the self by making it merely a collection of psychical states. John Stuart Mill says, in his Examination of Sir William Hamilton's Philosophy: "I could have abstained from murder if my aversion to the crime and my dread of its consequences had been weaker than the temptation which impelled me to commit it." [Footnote: Quoted by Bergson, Time and Free Will, p. 159 (Fr. p. 122).] Here desire, aversion, fear, and temptation are regarded as clear cut phenomena, external to the self which experiences them, and this leads to a curious balancing of pain and pleasure on purely utilitarian lines, turning the mind into a calculating machine such as one might find in a shop or counting-house, and taking no account of the character of the self that "wills." There is, really, in such a system of psychology, no room for self-expression, indeed, no meaning left for the term "self." It is only an inaccurate psychology, misled by language, which tries to show us the soul determined by sympathy, aversion, or hate, as though by so many forces pressing upon it from without. These feelings, provided that they go deep enough, make up the whole soul; in them the character of the individual expresses itself, since the whole content of the personality or soul is reflected in each of them. Then my character is "me." "To say that the soul is determined under the influence of any one of these feelings, is thus to recognize that it is self-determined. The associationist reduces the self to an aggregate of conscious states, sensations, feelings, and ideas. But if he sees in these various states no more than is expressed in their name, if he retains only their impersonal aspect, he may set them side by side for ever without getting anything but a phantom self, the shadow of the Ego, projecting itself into space. If, on the contrary, he takes these psychical states with the particular colouring which they assume in the case of a definite person, and which comes to each of them by reflection from all the others, then there is no need to associate a number of conscious states in order to rebuild the person, for the whole personality is in a single one of them, provided that we know how to choose it. And the outward manifestation of this inner state will be just what is called a free act, since the self alone will have been the author of it and since it will express the whole of the self." [Footnote: Time and Free Will, pp. 165-166 (Fr. pp. 126-127).] There is then room in the universe for a Freedom of the human Will, a definite creative activity, delivering us from the bonds of grim necessity and fate in which the physical sciences and the associationist psychology alike would bind us. Freedom, then, is a fact, and among the facts which we observe, asserts Bergson, there is none clearer. [Footnote: Time and Free Will, p. 221 (Fr. p. 169).] There are, however, one or two things which bear vitally upon the question of Freedom and which tend to obscure the issue. Of these, the foremost is that once we have acted in a particular manner we look back upon our actions and try to explain them with particular reference to their immediate antecedents. Here is where the mischief which gives rise to the whole controversy has its origin. We make static what is essentially dynamic in character. We call a process a thing. There is no such "thing" as Freedom; it is a relation between the self and its action. Indeed, it is only characteristic of a self IN ACTION, and so is really indefinable. Viewed after the action, it presents a different aspect; it has then become historical, an event in the past, and so we try to explain it as being caused by former events or conditions. This casting of it on to a fixed, rigid plan, gives action the appearance of having characteristics related to space rather than to time, in the real sense. As already shown in the previous chapter, this is due entirely to our intellectual habit of thinking in terms of space, by mathematical time, rather than in terms of living time or la duree.

Another point which causes serious confusion in the controversy is the notion that because, when an act has been performed, its antecedents may be reckoned up and their value and relative importance or influence assigned, this is equivalent to saying the actor could not have acted in any other way than he did, and, further, that his final act could have been foretold from the events which led up to it. It is a fact that in the realm of physical science we can foretell the future with accuracy. The astronomer predicts the precise moment and place in which Halley's comet will become visible from our earth. It is also a fact that we say of men and women who are our intimate friends: "I knew he (or she) would do such and such a thing" or "It's just like him." We base our judgment on our intimate acquaintance with the character of our friend, but this, as Bergson points out, "is not so much to predict the future conduct of our friend as to pass a judgment on his present character—that is to say, on his past." [Footnote: Time and Free Will, p. 184 (Fr. p. 140).] For, although our feelings and our ideas are constantly changing, yet we feel warranted in regarding our friend's character as stable, as reliable. But, as Mill remarked in his Logic: "There can be no science of human nature," because, although we trust in the reliability of our friend, although we have faith in his future actions, we do not, and cannot, know them. "Tout comprendre c'est tout pardonner." To say that, if we knew all the conditions, motives, fears, and temptations which led up to the actions of another, we could foretell what he would do, amounts to saying that, to do so, we should have actually to become that other person, and so arrive at the point where we act as he did because we are him. For Paul to foretell Peter's act, Paul would simply have to become Peter. [Footnote: Time and Free Will, p. 187 (Fr. p. 144).] The very reasons which render it possible to foretell an astronomical phenomenon are the very ones which prevent us from determining in advance an act which springs from our free activity. For the future of the material universe, although contemporaneous with the future of a conscious being, has no analogy to it. The astronomer regards time from the point of view of mathematics. He is concerned with points placed in a homogeneous time, points which mark the beginning or end of certain intervals. He does not concern himself with the interval in its actual duration. This is proved by the fact that, could all velocities in the universe be doubled, the astronomical formulae would remain unaffected, for the coincidences with which that science deals would still take place, but at intervals half as long. To the astronomer as such, this would make no difference, but we, in ourselves, would find that our day did not give us the full experience. Situations which arose as a result of the introduction of "summer time" serve to make this point clear. As then we find that time means two different things for the astronomer and the psychologist, the one being concerned with the points at the extremities of intervals, and the other with the enduring reality of the intervals themselves, we can see why astronomical phenomena are capable of prediction and see too that, for the same reason, events in the realm of human action cannot be so predicted and therefore the future is not predetermined but is being made.

Upon exactly parallel lines lie the references to causality in the controversy. In the physical realm events may recur, but in the mental realm the same thing can never happen again because we are living in real, flowing time, or la duree, and our conscious states are changing. Admitting that there is that in experience which warrants the application of the principle of causality, taking that principle as the statement that physical phenomena once perceived can recur, and that a given phenomenon, happening only after certain conditions, will recur when those precise conditions are repeated, [Footnote: See the brief paper Notre croyance a la loi de causalite, Revue de metaphysique et de morale, 1900.] still it remains open whether such a regularity of succession is ever possible in the human consciousness, and so the assertion of the principle of causality proves nothing against Freedom. We may admit that the principle is based on experience—but what kind of experience? Consideration of this question leads us to assert that the principle of causality only tends to accentuate the difference between objects in a realm wherein regular succession may be observed and predicted and a realm where it may not be observed or predicted, the realm of the self. Just because I endure and change I do not necessarily act to-day as I acted yesterday, when under like conditions. We do expect, however, that this will not be the case in the physical realm; for example, we expect that a flame applied to dry paper will always set it alight. Indeed, the more we realize the causal relation as one of necessary determination, we come to see that things do not exist as we do ourselves, and distinction between physical and psychical events becomes clear. We perceive that we, in ourselves, are centres of indetermination enjoying Freedom, and capable of creative activity.

We must, however, be careful to observe that such Freedom as we have is not absolute at all and that it admits of degrees. All our acts are by no means free. Indeed, Free Will is exceptional, and many live and die without having known true Freedom. Our everyday life consists in the performance of actions which are largely habitual or, indeed, automatic, being determined not by Free Will, but by custom and convention. Our Freedom is the exception and not the rule. Through sluggishness or indolence, we jog on in the even tenor of a way towards which habit has directed us. Even at times when our whole personality ought to vibrate, finding itself at the cross-roads, it fails to rise to the occasion. But, says Bergson, "it is at the great and solemn crises, decisive of our reputation with others, and yet more with ourselves, that we choose in defiance of what is conventionally called a motive, and this absence of any tangible reason, is the more striking the deeper our Freedom goes." [Footnote: Time and Free Will, p. 170 (Fr. p. 130).] At such times the self feels itself free and says so, for it feels itself to be creative. "All determinism will thus be refuted by experience, but every attempt to define Freedom will open the way to determinism." [Footnote: Time and Free Will, p. 330 (Fr. p. 177).]

It has been urged that, although Bergson is a stanch upholder of Freedom, it is Freedom of such a kind that it must be distinguished from Free Will, that is, from the liberty of choice which indeterminists have asserted and which determinists have denied; and that the Freedom for which he holds the brief is not the feeling of liberty that we have when confronted with alternative courses of action, or the feeling we have when we look back upon a choice made and an action accomplished, that we need not have acted as we did, and that we could have acted differently. Such Freedom it has been further maintained, is of little importance to us, for it is merely a free, creative activity which is the essence of life, which we share with all that lives and so cannot be styled "human" Freedom. Now, although many of Bergson's expressions, in regard to free, creative activity in general, lead to a connexion of this with the problem of "human" Freedom, such an identification would seem to be unfair. This seems specially so when we read over carefully his remarks about the coup d'etat of the fundamental self in times of grave crisis. We cannot equate this with a purely biological freedom or vitality, or spontaneity. But in the light of the criticism which has been made, it will be well to consider, in concluding this chapter, the statements made by Bergson in his article on Liberty in the work in connexion with the Vocabulaire philosophique for the Societe francaise de philosophie: [Footnote: Quoted by Le Roy in his Une nouvelle philosophie: Henri Bergson, English Translation (Benson), Williams and Norgate, p. 192.] "The word Liberty has for me a sense intermediate between those which we assign, as a rule, to the two terms 'Liberty' and 'Free Will.' On one hand I believe that 'Liberty' consists in being entirely oneself, in acting in conformity with oneself; it is then to a certain degree the 'moral liberty' of philosophers, the independence of the person with regard to everything other than itself. But that is not quite this Liberty, since the independence I am describing has not always a moral character. Further, it does not consist in depending on oneself as an effect depends on the cause which, of necessity, determines it. In this, I should come back to the sense of 'Free Will.'" And yet, he continues, "I do not accept this sense either, since Free Will, in the usual meaning of the term, implies the equal possibility of two contraries, and, on my theory, we cannot formulate or even conceive, in this case, the thesis of the equal possibility of the two contraries, without falling into grave error about the nature of Time. The object of my thesis has been precisely to find a position intermediate between 'moral Liberty' and 'Free Will.' Liberty, such as I understand it, is situated between these two terms, but not at equal distances from both; if I were obliged to blend it with one of the two, I should select 'Free-Will.'" Nor is Liberty to be reduced to spontaneity. "At most, this would be the case in the animal world where the psychological life is principally that of the affections. But in the case of a man, a thinking being, the free act can be called a synthesis of feelings and ideas, and the evolution which leads to it, a reasonable evolution." [Footnote: Matter and Memory, p. 243 (Fr. p. 205).] "In a word, if it is agreed to call every act free, which springs from the self, and from the self alone, the act which bears the mark of our personality is truly free, for our self alone will lay claim to its paternity." [Footnote: Time and Free Will, p. 172 (Fr. p. 132). It is interesting to compare with this the remark by Nietzsche in Also sprach Zarathustra, Thus Spake Zarathustra,—"Let your Ego be in relation to your acts that which the mother is in relation to the child."] The secret of the solution lies surely here, and in the words given above: "Liberty consists in being entirely oneself." If we act rightly we shall act freely, and yet be determined. Yet here there will be no contradiction, for we shall be self-determined. It is only the man who is self-determined that can in any sense be said to know the meaning of "human" Freedom. "We call free," said Spinoza, "that which exists in virtue of the necessities of its own nature, and which is determined by itself alone." Liberty is not absolute, for then we ourselves would be at the beck and call of every external excitation, desire, passion, or temptation. Our salvation consists in self-determination, so we shall avoid licence but preserve Freedom. We can only repeat the Socratic maxim—"Know thyself"—and resolve to take to heart the appeal of our own Shakespeare:

"To thine own self be true!"

CHAPTER VIII
EVOLUTION

Work of Darwin and Spencer—Bergson's L'Evolution creatrice—Life—L'elan vital—Evolution not progress in a straight line—Adaptation an insufficient explanation—Falsity of mechanistic view—Finalist conception of reality as fulfilling a plan false—Success along certain lines only—Torpor, Instinct, and Intelligence—Genesis of matter—Humanity the crown of evolution—Contingency and Freedom—The Future is being created.

Since the publication of Darwin's famous work on The Origin of Species in 1859, the conception of Evolution has become familiar and has won general acceptance in all thinking minds. Evolution is now a household word, but the actual study of evolutionary process has been the work of comparatively few. Science nowadays has become such a highly specialized affair, that few men cover a large enough field of study to enable them to deal effectively with this tremendous subject. What is more, those who shouted so loudly about Evolution as explaining all things have come to see that, in a sense, Evolution explains nothing by itself. Mere description of facts undoubtedly does serve a very useful purpose and may help to demolish some of the stanchly conservative theories still held in some quarters by those who prefer to take Hebrew conceptions as a basis of their cosmology however irreconcilable with fact these may prove to be. Mere description, however, is not ultimate, some philosophy of Evolution must be forthcoming. "Nowadays," remarks Hoffding, "every philosopher has to take up a position with respect to the concept of Evolution. It has now achieved its place among the categories or essential forms of thought by the fact of its providing indications whence new problems proceed. We must ask regarding every event, and every phenomenon, by what stages it has passed into its actual state. It is a special form of the general concept of cause. A philosophy is essentially characterized by the position which it accords to this concept and by the way in which it applies it." [Footnote: The Philosophy of Evolution—lecture IV, of Lectures on Bergson, in Modern Philosophers, Translated by Mason (MacMillan), p. 270.]

No one has done more to make familiar to English minds the notion of Evolution than Herbert Spencer. His Synthetic Philosophy had a grand aim, but it was manifestly unsatisfactory. The high hopes it had raised were followed by mingled disappointment and distrust. The secret of the unsatisfactoriness of Spencer is to be found in his method, which is an elaborate and plausible attempt to explain the evolution of the universe by referring the complex to the simple, the more highly organized to the less organized. His principle of Evolution never freed itself from bondage to mechanical conceptions.

Bergson's Creative Evolution, his largest and best known work, appeared in 1907. It has been regarded not only as a magnificent book, but as a date in the history of thought. Two of the leading students of evolutionary process in England, Professors Geddes and Thomson, refer to the book as "one of the most profound and original contributions to the philosophical consideration of the theory of Evolution." [Footnote: In the Bibliography in their volume Evolution.]

For some time there had been growing a need for an expression of evolutionary theory in terms other than those of Spencer, or of Haeckel—the German monistic philosopher. The advance in the study of biology and the rise of Neo-Vitalism, occasioned by an appreciation of the inadequacy of any explanation of life in terms purely physical and chemical, made the demand for a new statement, in greater harmony with these views, imperative. To satisfy this demand is the task to which Bergson has applied himself. He sounds the note of departure from the older conceptions right at the commencement by his very title, 'Creative' Evolution. For this, his views on Change, on Time, and on Freedom, have in some degree prepared us. We have seen set forth the fact of Freedom, the recognition of human beings as centres of indetermination, not mere units in a machine, "a block universe" where all is "given," but creatures capable of creative activity. Then by a consideration of Time, as la durée, we found that the history of an individual can never repeat itself; "For a conscious being, to exist is to change, to change is to mature, to mature is to go on creating oneself endlessly. Should the same be said," Bergson asks, "of existence in general?" [Footnote: Creative Evolution, p. 8 (Fr. p. 8).]

So he proceeds to portray with a wealth of analogy and brilliance of style, more akin to the language of a poet than a philosopher, the stupendous drama of Evolution, the mystery of being, the wonders of life. He makes the great fact of life his starting point. Is life susceptible to definition? We feel that, by the very nature of the case, it is not. A definition is an intellectual operation, while life is wider, richer, more fundamental than intellect. Indeed Bergson shows us that intellect is only one of the manifestations or adaptations of life in its progress. To define life, being strictly impossible, Bergson attempts to describe it. He would have us picture it as a great current emerging from some central point, radiating in all directions, but diverted into eddies and backwaters. Life is an original impetus, une poussee formidable, not the mere heading affixed to a class of objects which live. We must not speak any longer of life in general as an abstraction or a category in which we may place all living beings. Life, or the vital impulse, consists in a demand for creation, we might almost say "a will to create." It appears to be a current passing from one germ to another through the medium of a developed organism, "an internal push that has carried life by more and more complex forms, to higher and higher destinies." It is a dynamic continuity, a continuity of qualitative progress, a duration which leaves its bite on things. [Footnote: For these descriptions of life, see Creative Evolution, pp. 27-29 and 93-94 (Fr. pp. 28-30 and 95-96).] We shall be absolutely wrong, however, if we attempt to view the evolutionary process as progressive in a straight line. The facts contradict such a facile and shallow view. Some of the stock phrases of the earlier writers on Evolution were: "adaptation to environment," "selection" and "variation," and a grave problem was presented by this last. How are we to account for the variations of living beings, together with the persistence of their type? Herein lies the problem of the origin of species. Three different solutions have been put forward. There is the "Neo-Darwinian" view which attributes variation to the differences inherent in the germ borne by the individual, and not to the experience or behaviour of the individual in the course of his existence. Then there is the theory known as "Orthogenesis" which maintains that there is a continual changing in a definite direction from generation to generation. Thirdly, there is the "Neo-Lamarckian" theory which attributes the cause of variation to the conscious effort of the individual, an effort passed on to descendants. [Footnote: Concerning Lamarck (1744-1829) Bergson remarks in La Philosophie (1915) that without diminishing Darwin's merit Lamarck is to be regarded as the founder of evolutionary biology.] Now each one of these theories explains a certain group of facts, of a limited kind, but two difficulties confront them. We find that on quite distinct and widely separated lines of Evolution, exactly similar organs have been developed. Bergson points out to us, in this connexion, the Pecten genus of molluscs, which have an eye identical in structure with that of the eye of vertebrates. [Footnote: The common edible scallop (Pecten maximus) has several eyes of brilliant blue and of very complex structure.] It is obvious, however, that the eye of this mollusc and the eye of the vertebrate must have developed quite independently, ages after each had been separated from the parent stock. Again, we find that in all organic evolution, infinite complexity of structure accompanies the utmost simplicity of function. The variation of an organ so highly complex as the eye must involve the simultaneous occurrence of an infinite number of variations all co-ordinated to the simple end of vision. Such facts as these are incapable of explanation by reference to any or all of the three theories of adaptation and variation mentioned. Indeed they seem capable of explanation only by reference to a single original impetus retaining its direction in courses far removed from the common origin. "That adaptation to environment is the necessary condition of Evolution we do not question for a moment. It is quite evident that a species would disappear, should it fail to bend to the conditions of existence which are imposed on it. But it is one thing to recognize that outer circumstances are forces Evolution must reckon with, another to claim that they are the directing causes of Evolution." [Footnote: Creative Evolution, p. 107 (Fr. p. 111).]

"The truth is that adaptation explains the sinuosities of the movement of Evolution, but not the general directions of the movement, still less the movement itself. The road which leads to the town is obliged to follow the ups and downs of the hills; it adapts itself to the accidents of the ground, but the accidents of the ground are not the cause of the road nor have they given it its direction." [Footnote: Creative Evolution, p. 108 (Fr. p. 112).] The evolution of life cannot be explained as merely a series of adaptations to accidental circumstances. Moreover, the mechanistic view, where all is "given," is quite inadequate to explain the facts. The finalist or teleological conception is not any more tenable, for Evolution is not simply the realization of a plan. "A plan is given in advance. It is represented or at least representable, before its realization. The complete execution of it may be put off to a distant future or even indefinitely, but the idea is none the less formulable at the present time, in terms actually given. If, on the contrary, Evolution is a creation unceasingly renewed, it creates as it goes on, not only the forms of life but the ideas that enable the intellect to understand it. Its future overflows its present and cannot be sketched out therein, in an idea. There is the first error of finalism. It involves another yet more serious. If life realizes a plan it ought to manifest a greater harmony the further it advances, just as the house shows better and better the idea of the architect as stone is set upon stone." [Footnote: Creative Evolution, p. 108 (Fr. p. 112).] Such finalism is really reversed mechanism. If, on the contrary, the unity of life is to be found solely in the impetus (poussee formidable) that pushes it along the road of Time, the harmony is not in front but behind. The unity is derived from a vis a tergo: it is given at the start as an impulsion, not placed at the end as an attraction, as a kind of

"... far-off divine event

To which the whole creation moves."

"In communicating itself the impetus splits up more and more. Life, in proportion to its progress, is scattered in manifestations which undoubtedly owe to their common origin the fact that they are complementary to each other in certain aspects, but which are none the less mutually incompatible and antagonistic. So that the discord between species will go on increasing." "There are species which are arrested, there are some that retrogress. Evolution is not only a movement forward; in many cases we observe a marking-time, and still more often a deviation or turning back. Thence results an increasing disorder. No doubt there is progress, if progress means a continual advance in the general direction determined by a first impulsion; but this progress is accomplished only on the two or three great lines of Evolution on which forms ever more and more complex, ever more and more high, appear; between these lines run a crowd of minor paths in which deviations, arrests, and set-backs are multiplied." [Footnote: Creative Evolution, pp. 107-110 (Fr. pp. 111-114).] Evolution would be a very simple and easy process to understand if it followed one straight path. To describe it, Bergson uses, in one place, this metaphor: "We are here dealing with a shell which has immediately burst into fragments, which, being themselves species of shells, have again burst into fragments, destined to burst again, and so on." [Footnote: Creative Evolution, p. 103 (Fr. p. 107).]

A study of the facts shows us three very marked tendencies which may be denoted by the terms "Torpor," "Instinct," and "Intelligence." These are, in a sense "terminal points" in the evolutionary process. Hence arises the distinction of plant and animal, one showing a tendency to unconscious torpor, the other manifesting a tendency towards movement and consciousness. Then again arises another divergence which gives rise to two paths or tendencies, one along the line of the arthropods, at the end of which come the ants and the bees with their instincts, and the other along the line of the vertebrates, at the end of which is man with his intelligence. These three, Torpor, Instinct, and Intelligence, must not, however, be looked upon as three successive stages in the linear development of one tendency, but as three diverging directions of a common activity, which split up as it went on its way. Instinct and Intelligence are the two important terminal points in Evolution. They are not two stages of which one is higher than the other, they are at the end of two different roads. The wonders of Instinct are a commonplace to students of animal and insect life. [Footnote: See the interesting books by the French writer, Henri Fabre.] Men, with their intellect, make tools, while Instinct is tied to its tool. There is a wondrous immediacy, however, about Instinct, in the way it achieves ends, and its operations are often quite unconsciously performed. The insect or animal could not possibly "know" all that was involved in its action. Instinct, then, is one form of adaptation, while Intellect is quite another. In man — the grown man — Intellect is seen at its best. Yet we are not without Instincts; by them we are bound to the race and to the whole animal creation. But in ants and bees and such like creatures, Instinct is the sole guide of life, and it is often a highly organized life. The following example clearly shows the contrast between Instinct and Intelligence. A cat knows how to manage her new-born kittens, how to bring them up and teach them; a human mother does not know how to manage her baby unless she is trained either directly or by her own quick observation of other mothers. A cat performs her simple duties by Instinct, a human mother has to make use of her Intelligence in order to fulfil her very complex duties. We must observe, however, the relative value of Instinct and Intelligence. Each is a psychical activity, but while Instinct is far more perfect, far more complete in its insight, it is confined within narrow limits. Intelligence, while far less perfect in accomplishing its work, less complete in insight, is not limited in such a way. But while Intellect is external, looking on reality as different from life, Instinct is an inner sympathy with reality; it is deeper than any intellectual bond which binds the conscious creature to reality, for it is a vital bond.

Bergson now turns to a consideration of Life and Matter in the evolutionary process, and their precise relation to one another. Life is free, spontaneous, incalculable, not out of relation to Matter, but its direction is not entirely determined by Matter nor has its initial impulse Matter as its source. Although Bergson denies that Will and Consciousness, as we know them, are mere functions of the material organism, yet they do depend upon it as a workman depends upon his tool. We are fond of insinuating that a bad workman always blames his tools. A good workman, however, cannot be expected to do the best work with bad tools. The tool, although he uses it, at the same time limits him. So it is with the material organism at our disposal, our body, and so, too, with spirit and matter in general. Spirit and Matter are not to be regarded as independent or as ranged against one another from all eternity. Matter is a product of Spirit or Consciousness, the underlying psychic force. "For want of a better word," says Bergson, "we have called it Consciousness. But we do not mean the narrowed consciousness that functions in each of us." [Footnote: Creative Evolution, p. 250 (Fr. p. 258).] It is rather super-Consciousness than a consciousness like ours. Matter is a flux rather than a thing, but its flow is in the opposite direction to that of Spirit. The flow of Spirit shows itself in the creativeness of the evolutionary process; Matter is the inverse movement towards stability. Bergson adheres to the view of Spirit as fundamental, while Matter, he says, is due to a lessening of the tension of the spiritual force which is the initial elan. Now, of course, Matter and Spirit have come to be two opposing forces, for one is determined and the other free. Yet Bergson has to make out that there must have been some indetermination in Matter, however small, to give Spirit an opening to "insinuate itself" into Matter and thus use it for its own ends. It always seems, however, as if Spirit were trying to free itself from material limitations. It evolved the Intellect to cope with Matter. This is why Reason is at home, not in life and freedom, but in solid Matter, in mechanical and spatial distinctions. There is thus an eternal conflict in progress between Spirit and Matter. The latter is always tending to automatism, to the sacrifice of the Spirit with its creative power. In his little book on The Meaning of the War Bergson claims that here we have an instance of Life and Matter in conflict—Germany representing a mechanical and materialistic force. In quite another way he illustrates the same truth, in his book on Laughter, where he shows us that "rigidity, automatism, absent-mindedness, and unsociability, are all inextricably entwined, and all serve as ingredients to the making up of the comic in character," [Footnote: Laughter, p. 147 (Fr. p. 151).] for "the comic is that side of a person which reveals his likeness to a thing, that aspect of human events which, through its peculiar inelasticity, conveys the impression of pure mechanism, of automatism, of movement without life." [Footnote: Laughter, p. 87 (Fr. p. 89).]

Finally, in reviewing the evolutionary process as a whole, Bergson asserts that it manifests a radical contingency. The forms of life created, also the proportion of Intuition to Intelligence, in man, and the physique and morality of man, are all of them contingent. Life might have stored up energy in a different way through plants selecting different chemical elements. The whole of organic chemistry would then have been different. Then, too, it is probable that Life manifests itself in other planets, in other solar systems also, in forms of which we have no idea. He points out that between the perfect humanity and ours one may conceive many possible intermediaries, corresponding to all the degrees imaginable of Intelligence and Intuition. Another solution might have issued in a humanity either more intelligent or more intuitive. Man has warred like the other species, he has warred against the other species. If the evolution of life had been opposed by different accidents en route, if the current of life had been divided otherwise, we should have been, in physique and in morality, very different from what we are. [Footnote: Creative Evolution, pp. 280-282 (Fr. p. 288-290).] We cannot regard humanity as prefigured in the evolutionary process, nor look on man as the ultimate outcome of the whole of Evolution. The rest of Nature does not exist simply for the sake of man. Certainly man stands highest, for only in man has consciousness succeeded, but man has, as it were, lost much in coming to this position. The whole process of Evolution "IS AS IF A VAGUE AND FORMLESS BEING, WHOM WE MAY

CALL, AS WE WILL, man OR super-man, HAD SOUGHT TO REALIZE HIMSELF AND HAD SUCCEEDED ONLY BY ABANDONING A PART OF HIMSELF ON THE WAY." [Footnote: Creative Evolution, p. 281 (Fr. p. 289). (Italics are Bergson's.)]

In the lectures on The Nature of the Soul, Bergson referred to the "Pathway of the evolutionary process" as being a "Way to Personality." For on the line which leads to man liberation has been accomplished and thus personalities have been able to constitute themselves. If we could view this line of evolution it would appear to resemble a telegraph wire on which has travelled a dispatch sent off as long ago as the first beginnings of life, a message which was then confused, of which a part has been lost on the way, but which has at last found in the human race the appropriate instrument.

Humanity is one; we are members one of another. Bergson insists on this solidarity of man, and, indeed, of all living creatures. "As the smallest grain of dust is bound up with our entire solar system, drawn along with it in that undivided movement of descent which is materiality itself, so all organized beings, from the humblest to the highest, from the first origins of life to the time in which we are, and in all places as in all times, do but evidence a single impulsion, the inverse of the movement of matter, and in itself indivisible. All the living hold together and all yield to the same tremendous push. The animal takes its stand on the plant, man bestrides animality, and the whole of humanity, in space and in time, is one immense army galloping beside and before and behind each of us, in an overwhelming charge, able to beat down every resistance and clear the most formidable obstacles, perhaps even death." [Footnote: Creative Evolution, pp. 285-286 (Fr. pp. 293-294).]

CHAPTER IX
THE GOSPEL OF INTUITION

Intelligence and Intuition not opposed—Intellectual sympathy—Synthesis and analysis. "Understanding as one loves"—Concepts—Intellect not final—Man's spirit and intuitions—Joy, creative power and art—Value of Intuitive Philosophy.

We now approach the grand climax of Bergson's philosophy, his doctrine of Intuition, which he preaches with all the vigour of an evangelist. Our study of his treatment of Change, of Perception, of la duree, and of Instinct, has prepared us for an investigation of what he means by Intuition, for in dealing with these subjects he has been laying the foundations of his doctrine of Intuition. He pointed out to us that Life is Change, but that our intellect does not really grasp the reality of Change, for it is adapted to solids and to concepts, it resembles the cinematograph film. Then he has tried to show us that in Perception there is really much more than we think, for our intellect carves out what is of practical interest, while the penumbra or vague fringes of perceptions which have no bearing on action are neglected. By his advocacy of a real psychological Time, in opposition to the physical abstraction which bears the name, he again brought out the inadequacy of intellect to grasp Life in its flow and has put before us the soul's own appreciation of Time, which is a valuation rather than a magnitude, an intuition of our consciousness. Then, in examining the Evolution of Instinct and Intelligence, we found that Instinct, however blind intellectually, contained a wonderful and unique element of immediacy or direct insight. These are just preparatory indications of the direction of Bergson's thought all the time.

It is admittedly difficult to determine with very great definiteness what Bergson's view of Intuition really is, for he has made many statements regarding it which appear at first sight irreconcilable and, in his earlier writings, has not been sufficiently careful when speaking of the distinction between Intelligence and Intuition. Some of his early statements are reactionary and crude and give the impression of a purely anti-intellectualist position involving the condemnation of Intellect and all its work. [Footnote:

E.g., the statement "To philosophize is to invert the habitual direction of the work of thought" — Introduction to Metaphysics p. 59.] In his later work, however, Bergson has made it more clear that he does not mean to throw Intellect overboard; it has its place, but is not final, nor is it the supreme human faculty which most philosophers have thought it to be. It must be lamented, however, that Bergson's language was ever so ill defined as to encourage the many varied and conflicting views which are held regarding his doctrine of Intuition. Around this the greatest controversy has raged. Little is to be gained by heeding the shouts of either those who acclaim Bergson as a revolutionary against all use of the Intellect, or of those who regard him as no purely anti-intellectualist at all. We must turn to Bergson himself and study carefully what he has said and written, reserving our judgment until we have examined his own statements.

What is this "Intuition"? In what is now a locus classicus [Footnote: Introduction to Metaphysics, p. 7.] he says, "By Intuition is meant the kind of INTELLECTUAL SYMPATHY by which one places oneself within an object in order to coincide with what is unique in it and consequently inexpressible. Analysis is the operation which reduces the object to elements already known, that is, to elements common to it and other objects. To analyse, therefore, is to express a thing as a function of something other than itself. All analysis is thus a translation, a development into symbols, a representation taken from successive points of view from which we note as many resemblances as possible between the new object which we are studying and others which we believe we know already. In its eternally unsatisfied desire to embrace the object around which it is compelled to turn, analysis multiplies without end the number of its points of view in order to complete its always incomplete representation, and ceaselessly varies its symbols that it may perfect the always imperfect translation. It goes on therefore to infinity. But Intuition, if Intuition be possible, is a simple act. It is an act directly opposed to analysis, for it is a viewing in totality, as an absolute; it is a synthesis, not an analysis, not an intellectual act, for it is an immediate, emotional synthesis."

Two illustrations, taken from the same essay, may serve to make this point clearer. A visitor in Paris, of an artistic temperament, makes some sketches of the city, writing underneath them, by way of memento, the word "Paris." As he has actually seen Paris he is able, with the help of the original Intuition he has had of that unique whole which is Paris itself, to place his sketches therein, and synthesize them. But there is no way of performing the inverse operation. It is impossible, even with thousands of sketches, to achieve the Intuition, to give oneself the impression of what Paris is like, if one has never been there. Or again, as a second illustration,

"Consider a character whose adventures are related to me in a novel. The author may multiply the traits of his hero's character, may make him speak and act as much as he pleases, but all this can never be equivalent to the simple and indivisible feeling which I should experience if I were able, for an instant, to identify myself with the person of the hero himself. Out of that indivisible feeling, as from a spring, all the words, gestures, and actions of the man would appear to me to flow naturally. They would no longer be accidents which, added to the idea I had already formed of the character, continually enriched that idea without ever completing it. The character would be given to me all at once, in its entirety, and the thousand incidents which manifest it, instead of adding themselves to the idea and so enriching it, would seem to me, on the contrary, to detach themselves from it, without, however, exhausting it or impoverishing its essence. All the things I am told about the man provide me with so many points of view from which I can observe him. All the traits which describe him and which can make him known to me, only by so many comparisons with persons or things I know already, are signs by which he is expressed more or less symbolically. Symbols and points of view, therefore, place me outside him; they give me only what he has in common with others, and not what belongs to him, and to him alone. But that which is properly 'himself,' that which constitutes his essence, cannot be perceived from without, being internal by definition, nor be expressed by symbols, being incommensurable with everything else. Description, history, and analysis leave me here in the relative. Coincidence with the person himself would alone give me the absolute." [Footnote: An Introduction to Metaphysics, p. 3.] This, as Gaston Rageot puts it, is "to understand in the fashion in which one loves." This statement is of suggestive interest in considering the practical problem of how we may be said to "know" other people, and has vital bearing on the revelation of one personality to another, urging, as it does, the value and necessity of some degree of sympathy and indeed of love, for the full understanding and knowledge of any personality.

In another place Bergson says: "When a poet reads me his verses, I can interest myself enough in him to enter into his thought, put myself into his feelings, live over again the simple state he has broken into phrases and words. I sympathize then with his inspiration, I follow it with a continuous movement which is, like the inspiration itself, an undivided act." If this sympathy could extend its object and so reflect upon itself, it would give us the key to vital operations in the same way as Intelligence, developed and corrected, introduces us into Matter. Intelligence, by the intermediary of science, which is its work, tells more and more completely the secret of physical operations; of Life it gives and pretends only to give an expression in terms of inertia. We should be led into the very interior of Life by Intuition, that is, by Instinct become disinterested, conscious of itself, capable of reflecting on its object and enlarging it indefinitely.

In proclaiming the gospel of Intuition, Bergson's main point is to show that man is capable of an experience and a knowledge deeper than that which the Intellect can possibly give. "At intervals a soul arises which seems to triumph... by dint of simplicity—the soul of an artist or a poet, which, remaining near its source, reconciles, in a harmony appreciable by the heart, terms irreconcilable by the intelligence" [Footnote: From the address on Ravaisson, delivered before the Academie des Sciences morales et politiques 1904.] His point of view is here akin to that of an earlier French thinker, Pascal, who said: "The heart hath reasons that the reason cannot know." The Intellect is, by its nature, the fabricator of concepts, and concepts are, in Bergson's view, mischievous. They are static, they leave out the flux of things, they omit too much of experience, they are framed at an expensive cost, the expense of vital contact with Life itself. Of course he admits a certain value in concepts, but he refuses to admit that they help us at all to grasp reality in its flux. "Metaphysics must transcend concepts in order to reach Intuition. Certainly concepts are necessary to it, for all the other sciences work, as a rule, with concepts, and Metaphysics cannot dispense with the other sciences. But it is only truly itself when it goes beyond the concept, or at least when it frees itself from rigid and ready-made concepts, in order to create a kind very different from those which we habitually use; I mean supple, mobile, and almost fluid representations, always ready to mould themselves on the fleeting forms of Intuition." [Footnote: An Introduction to Metaphysics, p. 18.]

The true instrument of Metaphysics is intuition. We can only grasp ourselves, Bergson points out, by a metaphysical Intuition, for the soul eludes thought; we cannot place it among concepts or in a category. Intuition, however, reveals to us Real Time (la duree) and our real selves, changing and living as free personalities in a Time which, as it advances, creates.

Intuition is in no way mysterious, Bergson claims. Every one of us has had opportunities to exercise it in some degree, and anyone, for example, who has been engaged in literary work, knows perfectly well that after long study has been given to the subject, when all documents have been collected and necessary drafts worked out, one thing more is needful—an effort, a travail of soul, a setting of oneself in the heart of the subject; in short, the getting of inspiration. Metaphysical Intuition seems to be of this nature, and its relation to the empirical data contributed by the Intellect is parallel to the relation between the literary man's inspiration and his collected material. Of course "it is impossible to have an Intuition of reality, that is, an intellectual sympathy, with its innermost nature, unless its confidence has been won by a long comradeship with its external manifestation." In his study of Lucretius [Footnote: Extraits de Lucrece avec etude sur la poesie, la philosophie, la physique le texte et la langue de Lucrece (1884). Preface, p. xx.] he remarks that the chief value of the Latin poet-philosopher lay in his power of vision, in his insight into the beauty of nature, in his synthetic view, while at the same time he was able to exercise his keenly analytic intellect in discovering all he could about the facts of nature in their scientific aspect. At the same time, metaphysical Intuition, although only to be obtained through acquaintance with empirical data, is quite other than the mere summary of such knowledge. [Footnote: See protest: L'Intuition philosophique in Revue de metaphysique et de morale, 1911, p. 821.] It is distinct from these data, as the motor impulse is distinct from the path traversed by the moving body, as the tension of the spring is distinct from the visible movements of the pendulum. In this sense Metaphysics has nothing in common with a generalization of facts. It might, however, be defined as "integral experience." Nevertheless Intuition, once attained, must find a mode of expression in well-defined concepts, for in itself it is incommunicable. Dialectic is necessary to put Intuition to the proof, necessary also in order that Intuition should break itself up into concepts and so be propagated to others. But when we use language and concepts to communicate it, we tend to make these in themselves mean something, whereas they are but counters or symbols used to express what is their inspiration—Intuition. Hence we often forget the metaphysical Intuitions from which science itself has sprung. What is relative in science is the symbolic knowledge, reached by pre-existing concepts which proceed from the fixed to the moving. A truly intuitive philosophy would bring science and metaphysics together. Modern science dates from the day when mobility was set up as an independent reality and studied as such by Galileo. But men of science have mainly fixed their attention on the concepts, the residual products of Intuition, the symbols which have lent a symbolic character to every kind of science. Metaphysicians, too, have done the same thing. Hence it was easy for Kant to show that our science is wholly relative and our metaphysics entirely artificial. For Kant, science was a universal mathematic and metaphysics a practically unaltered Platonism. The synthetic Intuition was hidden by the analysis to which it had given rise. For Kant, Intuition was infra-intellectual, but for Bergson it is supra-intellectual. Kant's great error was in concluding that it is necessary for us, in order to attain Intuition, to leave the domain of the senses and of consciousness. This was because of his views of Time and Change. If Time and Change really were what he took them to be, then Metaphysics and Intuition alike are impossible. For Bergson, however, Time and Change lead up to Intuition; indeed it is by Intuition that we come to see all things, as he expresses it, sub specie durationis. This is the primary vision which an intuitive philosophy supplies. Such a philosophy will not be merely a unification of the sciences.

In an article contributed to the Revue de metaphysique et de morale in January of 1908, under the title L'Evolution de l'intelligence geometrique, we find Bergson remarking: "Nowhere have I claimed that we should replace intelligence by something else, or prefer instinct to it. I have tried to show merely that when we leave the region of physical and mathematical objects for the realm of life and consciousness, we have to depend on a certain sense of living, which has its origin in the same vital impulse that is the basis of instinct, although instinct, strictly speaking, is something quite different."

Intellect and Intuition, Bergson says very emphatically, at the close of his Huxley Lecture on Life and Consciousness, are not opposed to one another. "How could there be a disharmony between our Intuitions and our Science, how, especially, could our Science make us renounce our Intuition, if these Intuitions are something like Instinct—an Instinct conscious, refined, spiritualized—and if Instinct is still nearer Life than Intellect and Science? Intuition and Intellect do not oppose each other, save where Intuition refuses to become more precise by coming into touch with facts, scientifically studied, and where Intellect, instead of confining itself to Science proper (that is, to what can be inferred from facts, or proved by reasoning), combines with this an unconscious and inconsistent metaphysic which in vain lays claim to scientific pretensions. The future seems to belong to a philosophy which will take into account the whole of what is given." [Footnote: Life and Consciousness, as reported in The Hibbert Journal, Vol. X, Oct., 1911, pp. 24-44.] Intuition, to be fruitful, must interact with Intellect. It has the direct insight of Instinct, but its range is widened in proportion as it blends with Intellect. To imagine that the acceptance of the gospel of Intuition means the setting aside of all valuation in regard to the Intellect and its work would be preposterous. Bergson, however unguarded his language at times has been, does not mean this. He does not mean that we must return to the standpoint of the animal or that we must assume that the animal view, which is instinctive, is higher than the view which, through

Intellect, gives it a meaning and value to the percipient. That would involve the rejection of all that our culture has accumulated, all our social heritage from the past, the overthrow of our civilization, the undoing of all that has developed in our world, since man's Intelligence came into it. We cannot obtain Intuition without intellectual labour, for it must have an intellectual or scientific basis. Yet, however valuable Intellect is, it is not final. "It is reality itself, in the profoundest meaning of the word, that we reach by the combined and progressive development of science and philosophy." [Footnote: Creative Evolution, p. 210 (Fr. p. 217).] We need, therefore, if we are to get into touch with the deeper aspects of reality, something more than bare science. We cannot live on its dry bread alone; we need philosophy — an intuitional philosophy.

In his brilliant paper L'Intuition philosophique Bergson shows us, by a splendid study of Berkeley and Spinoza, that the great Intuition underlying the thought of a philosopher is of more worth to the world than the logic and dialectic through the aid of which it is made manifest, and elaborated. [Footnote: He makes this clear in a letter to Dr. Mitchell in the latter's Studies in Bergson's Philosophy, p. 31.] Then in the Lectures La Perception du Changement and in his little work on Laughter he sets forth the meaning of Intuition in relation to Art. From time to time Nature raises up souls more or less detached from practical life, seers of visions and dreamers of dreams, men of Intuition, with powers of great poetry, great music, or great painting. The clearest evidence of Intuition comes to us from the works of these great artists. What is it that we call the "genius" of great painters, great musicians, and great poets? It is simply the power they have of seeing more than we see and of enabling us, by their expressions, to penetrate further into reality ourselves. What makes the picture is the artist's vision, his entry into the subject by sympathy or Intuition, and however imperfectly he expresses this, yet he reveals to us more than we could otherwise have perceived.

The original form of consciousness, Bergson asserts, was nearer to Intuition than to Intelligence. But man has found Intellect the more valuable faculty for practical use and so has used it for the solution of questions it was never intended to solve, by reason of its nature and origin. Yet "Intuition is there, but vague and, above all, discontinuous. It is a lamp almost extinguished which only glimmers now and then for a few moments at most. But it glimmers whenever a vital interest is at stake. On our personality, on our liberty, on the place we occupy in the whole of Nature, on our origin, and perhaps also on our destiny, it throws a light, feeble and vacillating, but which, none the less, pierces the darkness of the night in which the Intellect leaves us." [Footnote: Creative Evolution, p. 282 (Fr. p. 290).]

Science promises us well-being, or, at the most, pleasure, but philosophy, through the Intuition to which it leads us, is capable of bestowing upon us Joy. The future belongs to such an intuitive philosophy, Bergson holds, for he considers that the whole progress of Evolution is towards the creation of a type of being whose Intuition will be equal to his Intelligence. Finally, by Intuition we shall find ourselves in — to invent a word — "intunation" with the elan vital, with the Evolution of the whole universe, and this absolute feeling of "at-one-ment" with the universe will result in that emotional synthesis which is deep Joy, which Wordsworth describes as:

> *"that blessed mood*
>
> *In which the burthen of the mystery,*
>
> *In which the heavy and the weary weight*
>
> *Of all this unintelligible world,*
>
> *Is lightened: — that serene and blessed mood,*
>
> *In which the affections gently lead us on, —*
>
> *Until, the breath of this corporeal frame*
>
> *And even the motion of our human blood*
>
> *Almost suspended, we are laid asleep*
>
> *In body, and become a living soul:*
>
> *While with an eye made quiet by the power*
>
> *Of harmony and the deep power of joy*
>
> *We see into the life of things."*

CHAPTER X
ETHICAL AND POLITICAL IMPLICATIONS

Anti-intellectualism and the State—Syndicalism—Class war, "direct action." Sorel advocates General Strike—Bergson cited in support—Unfair use of Bergson's view of reality—His ethic—Value of Will and Creativeness; not a supporter of impulse. Development of personality. Intuitive mind of woman. Change and the moral life.

Bergson has not written explicitly upon Ethics. In some quarters, however, so much has been made of Bergson as a supporter of certain ethical tendencies and certain social movements, that we must examine this question of ethical and political implications and try to ascertain how far this use of Bergson is justified.

Both ethical and political thought to-day are deriving fresh stimulation from the revision of many formulae, the modification of many conceptions which the War has inevitably caused. At the same time the keen interest taken in studies like social psychology and political philosophy combines with a growing interest in movements such as Guild Socialism and Syndicalism. The current which in philosophy sets against intellectualism, in the political realm sets against the State. This political anti-intellectualism shows a definite tendency to belittle the State in comparison with economic or social groups. "If social psychology tends to base the State as it is, on other than intellectual grounds, Syndicalism is prone to expect that non-intellectual forces will suffice to achieve the State as it should be." [Footnote: Ernest Barker in his Political Thought in England from Herbert Spencer to the Present Day, p. 248.] Other tendencies of the same type are noticeable. For example, Mr. Bertrand Russell's work on The Principles of Social Reconstruction is based on the view that impulse is a larger factor in our social life than conscious purpose.

The Syndicalists have been citing the philosophy of Bergson in support of their views, and it is most interesting to see how skilfully at times sayings of Bergson are quoted by them as authoritative, as justification for their actions, in a spirit akin to that of the devout man who quotes scripture texts as a guide to conduct.

In this country, Syndicalism has not been popular, and when it did show its head the government promptly prosecuted the editor and printers of its organ, The Syndicalist, and suppressed the paper owing to its aggressive anti-militarism. [Footnote: Imprisonment of Mr. Tom Mann] English Syndicalism has few supporters and it is a rather diluted form of French Syndicalism. To understand the movement, we must turn to its history in France or in America. Its history in Russia will be an object of research in the future, when more material and more news are available from that "distressful country." In France local unions or syndicats were legalized as early as 1884 but 1895 is the important landmark, being the date of the foundation with which Syndicalism is associated to-day, the Confederation Generale du Travail, popularly known as the "C.G.T.," the central trade-union organization in France. In the main, Syndicalism is an urban product, and has not many adherents among the agricultural population. In America a "Federation of Labour" was formed in 1886, but the Syndicalist organization there is the body known as "The Industrial Workers of the World." In its declaration of policy, it looks forward to a union which is to embrace the whole working class and to adopt towards the capitalist class an unending warfare, until the latter is expropriated. "The working class and the employing class," says the declaration, "have nothing in common. Between these two classes a struggle must go on until all the toilers come together on the industrial field and take and hold that which they produce by their labour." Among the leaders of Syndicalist thought on the Continent may be mentioned the names of three prominent Frenchmen, Berth, Lagardelle, and Sorel, together with that of the young Italian professor Labriola, who is leading the increasingly active party in his own country.

In France, Italy, and America alike, Syndicalism stands for the class-war. Its central feature is the idea of a General Strike. It manifests a hatred of the State, which makes it bitterly opposed to State Socialism, which it regards as centralized and tyrannical, or to a Labour-party of any kind in Parliament. [Footnote: Attempts at carrying out a General Strike, in France, Sweden, Italy, and Spain have failed. The greatest Strikes have been: Railwaymen in Italy, in 1907; Postal Workers in France, in 1909. Miners in New South Wales, in 1909, and in Sweden, 1909; Miners and Railwaymen in England; Textile Workers in Massachusetts, 1912; Railwaymen in England, 1919, in France, 1920.] It regards the State as fixed, rigid, and intellectual, and adopts all the Bergsonian anathemas it can find which condemn intellectual constructions, concepts, and thought in general. Its war-cry is not only "Down with Capitalism" but also, in a great number of cases, "Down with Intellectualism"! Instinct and impulse alone are to be guides. Syndicalism, unlike Socialism, has no programme—it does not believe in a prearranged plan. Reality, it says, quoting Bersgon, has no plan. It says, "Let us act, act instinctively and impulsively against what we feel to be wrong, and the future will grow out of our acting." We find Georges Sorel, the philosopher of Syndicalism, talking about what he terms the INTUITION of Socialism, and he talks emphatically about the tremendous moral value of strikes, apart from any material gain achieved by them. He believes religiously in a General Strike as the great ideal, but considers it a myth capable of rousing enthusiasm in the workers, an ideal to which they must strive, a myth as inspiring as the belief of the early Christians in the Second Coming of Christ, which, although quite a false belief, contributed largely to the success of the early Church. "Strikes," says Sorel, "have engendered in the proletariat the most noble, the most profound, the most moving sentiments they possess. The General Strike groups these in a composite picture, and by bringing together, gives to each its maximum intensity; appealing to the most acute memories of particular conflicts, it colours with an intense life all the details of the composition presented to the mind. We obtain thus an intuition of Socialism which language cannot clearly express and we obtain it in a symbol instantly perceived, such as is maintained in the Bergsonian philosophy." [Footnote: Quoted by C. Bougle, in an interesting article Syndicalistes et Bergsoniens, Revue du mois, April 10, 1909. And by Rev. Rhondda Williams in Syndicalism in France and its Relation to the Philosophy of Bergson, Hibbert Journal, 1914. Also by J. W. Scott in his book Syndicalism and Philosophical Realism, 1919, pp. 39-40, and by Harley in Syndicalism.] In England, although the idea of the General Strike has not been so prominent, yet in recent years Strikes have assumed an aspect different from those of former years. Workers who had "struck" before for definite objects, for wages or hours, or reformed workshop conditions, now seem to be seeking after something vaster—a fundamental alteration in industrial conditions or the total abolition of the present system. The spirit of unrest is on the increase; no doubt War conditions have, in many cases, intensified it, but there is in the whole industrial world an instinctive impulse showing itself, which is issuing in Syndicalist and Bolshevist [Footnote: "Bolshevik"—simply the Russian word for majority party as distinct from Mensheviks or minority.] activities of various kinds. Syndicalism is undoubtedly revolutionary. There are Les Syndicats rouges and Les Syndicats jaunes, of which the "Reds" are by far the most revolutionary. [Footnote: See article Des Ouvriers syndiques et le Syndicalisme jaune, Revue de metaphysique et morale, 1912] The C.G.T. and the Industrial Workers of the World are out for what they call "direct action." Their anarchy is really an organization directed against organization, at least against that organization we know as the modern State. They have no hope of salvation for themselves coming about through the State in any way. It has become somewhat natural for us to think of the social reformer as a Member of Parliament and of the revolutionary socialist as a "strike-agitator." The cries of "Don't vote!" "Don't enlist!" are heard, and care is taken to keep the workman from ceasing to quarrel with his employer. Any discussion of the rights or wrongs of any Strike is condemned at once. [Footnote: Ramsay MacDonald was condemned by the Syndicalists for claiming that a strike MIGHT be wrong.] All Strikes are regarded as right and as an approach to the ideal of the General Strike. Sorel cites Bergson as calling us to turn from traditional thought, to seek reality in the dynamic, rather than the static. He claims that the Professor of Philosophy at the College de France really co-operates with the C.G.T. An unexpected harmony arises "between the flute of personal meditation, and the trumpet of social revolution, and the workman is inspired by being made to feel that the elan ouvrier est frere de l'elan vital." [Footnote: Quoted by C. Bougie in the article previously mentioned.] As Bergson speaks of all movement as unique and indivisible, so the triumphant movement of the General Strike is to be regarded as a whole, no analysis is to be made of its parts. As the portals of the future stand wide open, as the future is being made, so Bergson tells us, that is deemed an excuse by the Syndicalists for having no prearranged plan of the conduct of the General Strike, and no conception of what is to be done afterwards. It is unforeseen and unforeseeable. All industries, however, are to be in the hands of those who work them, the present industrial system is to be swept away. The new order which is to follow will have entirely new moral codes. Sorel justifies violence to be used against the existing order, but says he wishes to avoid unnecessary blood-shed or brutality. [Footnote: Reflections on Violence. It is interesting to note that Bergson refers briefly to Sorel as an original thinker whom it is impossible to place in any category or class, in La Philosophie, p. 13.] He remarks however, in this connexion, that ancient society, with all its brutality, compares favourably with modern society which has replaced ferocity by cunning. The ancient peoples had less hypocrisy than we have; this, in his opinion, justifies violence in the overthrow of the modern system and the creation of a nobler ethic than that on which the modern State is based. For this reason, he disagrees with most of his Syndicalist colleagues, and condemns sabotage and also the ca canny policy, both of which are a kind of revenge upon the employer, based on the principle of "bad work for bad pay." He would have the workers produce well now, and urges that moral progress is to be aimed at no less than material progress.

It certainly seems, however, that the Syndicalists are making an unfair use of Bergson. They have got hold of three or four points rather out of relation to their context, and are making the most of them. These points are, chiefly, his remarks against the Intellect, his appreciation of Instinct and Intuition, his insistence on Freedom and on the Indeterminateness of the Future. In the hands of the Syndicalists these become in effect: "Never mind what you think, rouse up your feeling intensely; act as you feel and then see what you think." Briefly this amounts to saying: "Act on impulse, behave instinctively and not rationally." In too many cases, as we know, this is equivalent to a merely selfish "Down tools if you feel like it." Now so far from Bergson really giving any countenance to capricious behaviour, or mere impulse, he expressly condemns such action. Although the future is being made, he does not admit that it will be merely CAPRICIOUSLY made, and he condemns the man of mere impulse along with the dreamer, in a fine passage where he speaks of the value of an intelligent memory in practical life.[Footnote: See p. 48 of the present work.] When the Syndicalists assert that elan, instinct, impulse, or intuition are a better guide than intelligence and reasoned principles, and cite Bergson as their authority, they omit an important qualification which upsets their theory entirely, for Bergson's anti-intellectualism is not at all of the type which they advocate. He does not intend to rule Intellect out of practical affairs. Indeed it is just the opposite that he asserts, for, in his view, the Intellect is pre-eminently fitted for practical life, for action, and it is for this very reason that he maintains it does not give us insight into reality itself, which Intuition alone can do. He does not wish, however, to decrease the small element of rationality manifested in ethical and political life, least of all to make men less rational, in the sense that they are to become mere creatures of Impulse.

Nevertheless, Bergson's great emphasis on Will and Creativeness condemns any laissez-faire type of political theory. It would be wrong for us to accept the social order which is felt to be imperfect and unjust in so many ways, simply because we find ourselves in it and fear we cannot work a way out. WE HAVE GREAT POWER OF CREATION, AND IN LARGE MEASURE WE CAN CREATE WHAT WE WILL IN THE WORLD OF POLITICS AND SOCIAL LIFE, and it is good that men generally should be made to see this. But it is of very vital importance that we should will the right thing. This we are not likely to do impulsively and without reflection. Even if we admit Mr. Russell's contention that "impulse has more effect than conscious purpose in moulding men's lives" [Footnote: Principles of Social Reconstruction, Preface, p. 5.] and agree that "it is not the weakening of impulse that is to be desired, but the direction of impulse toward life and growth," [Footnote: p. 18. Cf. the whole of the first chapter on The Principle of Growth.] yet, we none the less assert that instinct is an insufficient guide in the determination of social behaviour, and ask how the direction of impulse, of which Mr. Russell himself speaks, is to be arrived at? Surely our only hope lies in striving to make men not less, but more rational in order that they may grasp—however dimly—something of what is implied in ethical and political ideals, that they may recognize in society some embodiment of will and purpose and come to look upon Thought and Reason as the unifying and organizing principles of human society.

We cannot help wishing that Bergson had given us some contribution to the study of Ethics. In one of his letters to Father de Tonquedec regarding the relation of his philosophy to Theology, we find him remarking that "Before these conclusions [theological statements] can be set out with greater precision, or considered at greater length, certain problems of quite another kind would have to be attacked—the problems of Ethics. I am not sure that I shall ever publish anything on this subject. I shall do so only if I attain the results that appear to me as demonstrable or as clearly to be shown as those of my other books." [Footnote: In Etudes (Revue des Peres de Jesus), Vol. CXXX, pp. 514, 515, 1912.] Prior to the War, however, we know that Bergson was taking up the problem of working out the implications of his philosophy in the sphere of social ethics, with particular reference to the meaning of "Duty" and the significance of "Personality." Although his investigations of these supremely important problems have not yet been completed or made public, nevertheless certain ethical implications which have an important bearing on personal and social life seem to be contained in what he has already written.

In its application to social life, Bergson's philosophy would involve the laying of greater stress upon the need for all members of society having larger opportunities of being more fully themselves, of being self-creative and having fuller powers of self-expression as free creative agents. It would lay emphasis upon the value of the personality of the worker and would combat the systematic converting of him into a mere "hand." Thus would be set in clearer light the claims of human personality to create and to enjoy a good life in the widest sense, to enter into fuller sympathy and fellowship with other personalities, and so develop a fuller and richer form of existence than is possible under present social and industrial conditions. It would mean a transvaluation of all social values, an esteeming of personality before property, a recognition of material goods as means to a good life, when employed in the social service of the spirit of man. It would involve a denunciation of the enslavement of man's spirit to the production of material wealth. Each man would be a member of a community of personalities, each of unique value, treating each other, not as means to their own particular selfish ends, but as ends in themselves. At the same time it would involve the putting of the personality of the citizen in the foremost place in our social and political life, instead of a development of a purely class consciousness with its mischievous distinctions.

Articles have been written dealing with Bergson's message to Feminism. This point is not without its importance in our modern life. It must be admitted that the present system of civilization with its scientific campaign of conquest of the material environment has been the work of man's intellect. In the ruder stages of existence women's subordination to men may have been necessary and justifiable. But in the development of society it has become increasingly less necessary, and humanity is now at a stage where the contributions of women to society are absolutely vital to its welfare and progress. Woman is proverbially and rightly regarded as more intuitive than man. This need not be taken to mean that, given the opportunity of intellectual development (until now practically denied to her), woman would not show as great ability in this direction as man. But it is an undeniable fact that woman has kept more closely to the forces of the great life-principle, both by the fact that in her rests the creative power for the continuation of the human family and also by the fact that the development of the personalities of children has been her function. The subjection in which women have been largely kept until now has not only hindered them from taking part in the work of society as a whole and from expressing their point of view, but has meant that many of them have little or no knowledge of their capacities and abilities in wider directions. However, with their increasing realization of their own powers, with the granting of increased opportunities to them, and an adequate recognition of their personality side by side with that of men, achievements of supreme value for humanity as a whole may be expected from them. In certain spheres they may be found much better adapted than are men to achieve a vision which will raise human life to a higher plane and give it greater worth. More especially in the realms of ethical development, of social science, problems of sex, of war and peace, of child welfare, health, and education, of religion and philosophy we may hope to have valuable contributions from the more intuitive mind of woman. "It is not in the fighting male of the race: it is in Woman that we have the future centre of Power in civilization." [Footnote: Benjamin Kidd in The Science of Power, p. 195. This is more fully shown in his chapters, Woman the Psychic Centre of Power in the Social Integration, and The Mind of Woman, pp. 192-257.] The wandering Dante required for his guidance not only the intellectual faculties of a Vergil but in addition the intuitive woman-soul of a Beatrice to lead him upward and on.

In La Conscience et la Vie [Footnote: L'Energie spirituelle, p. 27 (Mind-Energy).] Bergson indicates slightly his views on SOCIAL evolution—c'est a la vie sociale que l'evolution aboutit, comme si le besoin s'en etait fait sentir des le debut, ou plutot comme si quelque aspiration originelle et essentielle de la vie ne pouvait trouver que dans la societe sa pleine satisfaction. He seems inclined to turn his attention to the unity of life, not simply as due to an identity of original impulse but to a common aspiration. There is involved a process of subordination and initiative on the part of the individual. The existence of society necessitates a certain subordination, while its progress depends on the free initiative of the individual. It is extremely dangerous for any society, whether it be an International League, a State, either Communistic or Capitalistic, a Trade Union, or a Church, to suppress individual liberty in the interests of greater social efficiency or of increased production or rigid uniformity of doctrine. With the sacrifice of individual initiative will go the loss of all "soul," and the result will be degeneration to a mechanical type of existence, a merely stagnant institution expressing nothing of man's spirit. This personal power of initiative Bergson appeals to each one to maintain. In an important passage of his little work on Laughter he makes a personal moral appeal.

"What life and society require of each of us is a constantly alert attention, that discerns the outlines of the present situation, together with a certain elasticity of mind and body to enable us to adapt ourselves in consequence." [Footnote: Laughter, p. 18 (Fr. p. 18).] The lack of tension and elasticity gives rise to mental deficiency and to grave inadaptability which produces misery and crime. Society demands not only that we live but that we live well. This means that we must be truly alive; for Bergson, the moral ideal is to keep spiritually alert. We must be our real, living selves, and not hide behind the social self of hypocrisy and habit. We must avoid being the victims of mechanism or automatism. We must avoid at all costs "getting into a rut" morally or spiritually. Change and vision are both necessary to our welfare. Where there is no vision, no undying fire of idealism, the people perish.

Resistance to change is the sin against the Holy Spirit. Bergson is opposed to the conventional view of morality as equivalent to rigidity, and grasps the important truth that if morality is to be of worth at all it must lie not in a fixed set of rules, habits, or conventions, but in a spirit of living. This is of very great ethical importance indeed, as it means that we must revise many of our standards of character. For example, how often do we hear of one who, holding an obviously false view long and obstinately, is praised as consistent, whereas a mind which moves and develops with the times, attempting always to adjust itself to changing conditions in its intellectual or material environment, is contemptuously dubbed as "changeable" by the moralists of rigidity. We must, however, learn that consistency of character does not mean lack of change. Stanchness of character is too often mere obstinate resistance to change. We must therefore be on our guard against those who would run ethics into rigid moulds, and so raise up static concepts and infallible dogmas for beliefs or action. Change must be accepted as a principle which it is both futile and immoral to ignore, even in the moral life. This does not mean setting up caprice or impulsiveness, for in so far as our change of character expresses the development of the single movement of our own inner life it will be quite other than capricious, but it will be change, and a change which is quite consistent, a creative evolution of our personality.

No merely materialistic ethic can breathe in the atmosphere of Bergson's thought, which sets human consciousness in a high place and insists upon the fact of Freedom. He maintains a point of view far removed from the old naturalistic ethic; he does take some account of "values," freedom, creativeness, and joy (as distinct from pleasure). He points out that Matter, although to a degree the tool of Spirit, is nevertheless the enemy who threatens us with a lapse into mere automatism which is only the parody of true life. The eternal conflict of Matter and Spirit in Evolution demands that we place ourselves on the side of spiritual rather than merely material values. We must not be like "the man with the muck rake." Our conceptions of goodness must be not merely static but dynamic, for the moral life is essentially an evolution—"a growth in grace." It means a constant "putting on of the new man," never "counting oneself to have attained," for spirituality is a progress to ever new creations, the spiritual life is an unending adventure, and is, moreover, one which is hampered and crushed by all refusals to recognize that Change is the fundamental feature of the universe. Nothing can be more mischievous, more detrimental to moral progress—which is ultimately the only progress of value and significance to humanity—than the deification of the status quo either in the individual or in society as a whole.

CHAPTER XI
RELATION TO RELIGION AND THEOLOGY

Avoidance of theological terms — Intuition and faith — God and Change — Deity not omnipotent but creative and immanent — God as "Creator of creators" — Problem of teleology — Stimulus to theology — The need for restatements of the nature of God — Men as products and instruments of divine activity — Immortality.

We have seen that Bergson holds no special brief for science, for, as has been shown, he opposes many of the hypotheses to which science clings. Consequently, some persons possessing only a superficial acquaintance with Bergson, and having minds which still think in the exclusive and opposing terms of the conflict of science and religion of a generation past, have enthusiastically hailed him as an ally of their religion. We must examine carefully how far this is justifiable. It is perfectly natural and just that many people, unable to devote time or energy to the study of his works, want to know, in regard to Bergson, as about every other great thinker, what is the bearing of his thought on their practical theory of life, upon their ideals of existence, upon the courage, faith, and hope which enable them to work and live, feeling that life is worth while. We must, however, guard against misuse of Bergson, particularly such misuse of him as that made in another sphere, by the Syndicalists. We find that in France he has been welcomed by the Modernists of the Roman Catholic Church as an ally, and by not a few liberal and progressive Christian theologians in this country.

At the outset, we must note that Bergson avoids theological forms of expression, because he is well aware that these — especially in a philosophical treatise — may give rise to misconceptions. He does not, like Kant, attack any specific or traditional argument for Theism; he does not enter into theological controversy. He has not formulated, with any strictness, his conception of God; for he has recognized that an examination of Theism would be of little or no value, which was not prefaced by a refutation of mechanism and materialism, and by the assertion of some spiritual value in the universe. It is to such a labour that Bergson has applied himself; it is only incidentally that we find him making remarks on religious or theological conceptions. His whole philosophy, however, involves some very important religious conceptions and theological standpoints. In France, Bergson has had a considerable amount of discussion on the theological implications of his philosophy with the Jesuit Fathers, notably Father de Tonquedec. These arise particularly from his views concerning Change, Time, Freedom, Evolution and Intuition.

Bergson has been cited as a "Mystic" because he preaches a doctrine of Intuition. But his metaphysical Intuition bears no relation to the mysticism of the saint or of the fervid religious mind. He expressly says, "The doctrine I hold is a protest against mysticism since it professes to reconstruct the bridge (broken since Kant) between metaphysics and science." Yet, if by mysticism one means a certain appeal to the inner and profound life, then his philosophy is mystical—but so is all philosophy. We must beware of any attempts to run Bergson's thought into moulds for which it was never intended, and guard against its being strained and falsely interpreted in the interests of some special form of religious belief. Intuition is not what the religious mind means by Faith, in the accepted sense of belief in a doctrine or a deity, which is to be neither criticized nor reasoned about. Religion demands "what passeth knowledge." Furthermore, it seeks a reality that abides above the world of Change, "The same yesterday, to-day, and for ever," to which it appeals. The religious consciousness finds itself most reluctant to admit the reality of Change, and this, we must remember, is the fundamental principle of Bergson's thought. Faber, one of the noblest hymn writers, well expresses this attitude:

"O, Lord, my heart is sick,

Sick of this everlasting change,

And Life runs tediously quick

Through its unresting race and varied range.

Change finds no likeness of itself in Thee,

And makes no echo in Thy mute eternity."

For Bergson, God reveals Himself in the world of Time, in the very principle of Change. He is not "a Father of lights in Whom is no variableness nor shadow of turning."

It has been said that the Idea of God is one of the objects of philosophy, and this is true, if, by God, we agree to mean the principle of the universe, or the Absolute. Unity is essential to the Idea of God. For the religious consciousness, of course, God's existence is a necessary one, not merely contingent. It views Him as eternal and unchangeable. But if we accept the Bergsonian philosophy, God cannot be regarded as "timeless," or as "perfect" in the sense of being "eternal" and "complete." He is, so to speak, realizing Himself in the universe, and is not merely a unity which sums up the multiplicity of time existence. Further, He must be a God who acts freely and creatively and who is in time. Trouble has arisen in the past over the relation of "temporal" and "eternal" — the former being regarded as appearance. For Bergson, this difficulty does not arise; there is, for him, no such dualism. His God is not exempt from Change, He is not to be conceived as existing apart from and independent of the world. Indeed, for him, God would seem to be merely a focus imaginarius of Life and Spirit, a "hypostatization" of la duree. He cannot be regarded as the loving Father of the human race whom He has begotten or created in order that intelligent beings "may glorify Him and enjoy Him for ever." Bergson does not offer us a God, personal, loving, and redemptive, as the Christian religious consciousness demands or imagines. He does not, and can not, affirm Christian Theism, for he considers that the facts do not warrant the positing of a self-conscious and personal Individual in the only sense in which we, from our experience, can understand these words. God is pure, creative activity, a flowing rather than a fountain head; a continuity of emanation, not a centre from which things emanate. For Bergson, God is anthropomorphic — as He must necessarily be for us all — but Bergson's is anthropomorphism of a subtle kind. His God is the duree of our own conscious life, raised to a higher power. Dieu se fait in the evolutionary process. He is absolutely unfinished, not complete or perfect. He is incessant life, action, freedom, and creativeness, and in so far as we ourselves manifest these (seen, above all, in the creative joy of the inventor, poet, artist, and mother) each of us has the "divine" at work within. For Bergson, God is a Being immanent in the universe, but He is ignorant of the direction in which Evolution is progressing. This is not the God of the ordinary religious consciousness, nor is it a conception of God which satisfies the limited notion which our own imagination both creates and craves to find real. God, it would seem, must be greater than His works, and He must know what He is doing. It has been objected that a force, even if a divine force (one can hardly call it "God" in the ordinary meaning of that vague word) which urges on Matter without knowing in what direction or to what end, is no God at all, for it is merely personified chance. This is due to what Hegel calls "the error of viewing God as free." [Footnote: Logic, Wallace's translation, first edition, p. 213.]

In reply to certain criticisms of his book L'Evolution creatrice made by Father de Tonquedec, Bergson wrote in 1912: "I speak of God as the source whence issue successively, by an effort of his freedom, the currents or impulses each of which will make a world; he therefore remains distinct from them, and it is not of him that we can say that 'most often it turns aside' or is 'at the mercy of the materiality that it has been bound to adopt.' Finally, the reasoning whereby I establish the impossibility of 'nothing' is in no way directed against the existence of a transcendent cause of the world; I have, on the contrary, explained that this reasoning has in view the Spinozist conception of Being. It issues in what is merely a demonstration that 'something' has always existed. As to the nature of this 'something' it is true that nothing in the way of a positive conclusion is conveyed. But neither is it stated in any fashion that what has always existed is the world itself, and the rest of the book explicitly affirms the contrary." [Footnote: Tonquedec: Dieu dans l'Evolution creatrice (Beauchesne), and Annales de philosophie chretienne, 1912.] "Now the considerations set forth in my Essai sur les donnees immediates result in bringing to light the fact of freedom, those of Matiere et Memoire point directly, I hope, to the reality of Spirit, those of L'Evolution creatrice exhibit creation as a fact. From all this emerges clearly the idea of a God, creator and free, the generator of both Matter and Life, whose work of creation is continued on the side of Life by the evolution of species and the building up of human personalities. From all this emerges a refutation of monism and of pantheism." [Footnote: Tonquedec: Dieu dans l'Evolution creatrice (Beauchesne), and also Etudes des Peres de Jesus, Vol. CXXX, 1912.] To this it was replied that, for Catholic theology, God is not merely the source from which the river springs, God does not develop Himself to a world but He causes it to appear by a kind of creation quite different from that of Bergson. Bergson's God is not the God of pantheism, because, for him, the Deity is immanent in nature, not identifiable with it. A true account of the Absolute would, for him, take the form of history. Human history has a vital meaning for him. God is not omnipotent; He is a fighter who takes sides. He is not a "potter-God" with a clay world. The world involves a limiting of God, and theology has always found this its most difficult problem, for the evils or defects against which the Creator is waging war are evils and defects in a world of His own creating. Speaking in 1914, at the Edinburgh Philosophical Society, Bergson remarked that God might be looked upon as "a Creator of creators." Such a view, more explicitly worked out, might bring him into line with the religious attempt to reconcile the divine action with our own work and freedom. Our wills are ours, but in some mystic way religion believes they may become His also, and that we may be "fellow-labourers together with God." The religious view of the perfection of the Divine, its omniscience and omnipotence, has always been hard to reconcile with free will. Christian theology, when based on the perfection of the Divine nature, has always tended to be determinist. Indeed, free will has been advocated rather as an explanation of the presence of evil (our waywardness as in opposition to the will of God) than as the privilege and necessary endowment of a spiritual being, and so the really orthodox religious mind has been forced to seek salvation in self-surrender and has found consolation in reliance on the "grace" or "active good will" of God. Thus many theologians in an attempt to reconcile this with human freedom speak mystically, nevertheless confidently, of "the interaction of Grace and Free-Will."

The acceptance of Creative Evolution involves the acceptance of a God who expresses Himself in creative action called forth by changing situations. It cannot regard Evolution as merely the unrolling in time of the eternally complete, as in the view of monistic idealism. We find in Bergson, however, two hints which suggest that some vague idealistic conception has been present to his mind. For instance, in speaking of Time in relation to God, we find him suggesting that "the whole of history might be contained in a very short time for a consciousness at a higher degree of tension than our own, which should watch the development of humanity while contracting it, so to speak, into the great phases of its evolution." [Footnote: Matter and Memory, p. 275 (Fr. p. 231).] This remark seems an echo of the words of the old Hebrew poet:

> *"For a thousand years in Thy sight*
>
> *Are but as yesterday when it is past,*
>
> *And as a watch in the night."*

Again, in L'Evolution creatrice we find him suggesting that in maternity and love may lie the secret of the universe.

The important point however, in considering Bergson in relation to Religion and Theology, is his marked objection to teleology. It is this which has led many to style his philosophy pessimistic. Religion does not live readily in a pessimistic atmosphere. Then religion regards Life and the Universe as valuable, not because they yield to some single impulsion, but because, at every step, they manifest a meaning and significance interpreted by our conceptions of value. Bergson's view only favours religion as ordinarily comprehended, in so far as it breaks away from a materialistic mechanism, and asserts freedom and gives Spirit some superiority over Matter. At first sight, the term "creative" seemed very promising, but can we stop where Bergson has left us? Why should he banish teleology? His super-consciousness is so indeterminate that it is not allowed to hamper itself with any purpose more definite than that of self-augmentation. The course and goal of Evolution are to it unknown and unknowable. Creation, freedom, and will are great things, as Mr. Balfour remarks, but we cannot lastingly admire them unless we know their drift. It is too haphazard a universe which Bergson displays. Joy does not seem to fit in with what is so aimless. It would be better to invoke God with a purpose than a supra-consciousness with none. [Footnote: Creative Evolution and Philosophic Doubt, Hibbert Journal, Oct., 1911, pp. 1-23.]

In response to an international inquiry, conducted by Frederic Charpin, for the Mercure de France, formulated in the question, Assistons-nous a une dissolution ou a une evolution de l'idee religieuse et du sentiment religieux? Bergson wrote: "I feel quite unable to foretell what the external manifestation of the religious sense may be in time to come. I can only say that it does not seem to me likely to be disintegrated. Only that which is made up of parts can be disintegrated. Now, I am willing to admit that the religious sense has been gradually enriched and complicated by very diverse elements; none the less it is in essence a simple thing, sui generis; and resembles no other emotion of the soul. It may, perhaps be urged that a simple element, although it cannot be decomposed, may yet disappear, and that the religious sense will inevitably vanish when it has no object to which it can attach itself. But this would be to forget that the object of the religious sense is, in part at least, prior to that sense itself; that this object is felt even more than it is thought and that the idea is, in this case, the effect of the feeling quite as much as its cause. The progressive deepening of the idea may therefore make the religious sense clearer and ever clearer; it cannot modify that which is essential in it, still less effect its disappearance." [Footnote: Charpin: La Question religieuse, 1908, Paris.]

We find Bergson reported as believing that the individual cannot be guided solely by considerations of a purely moral character. Morality, even social ethics, is not enough in view of the longing for religious experience, the yearning for at least a feeling of definite relationship between the individual human personality and the great spiritual source of life. This is a feeling which he believes will grow. [Footnote: New York Times, Feb. 22, 1914.]

Bergson's philosophy has aroused a new interest in many theological questions. The dogmas of theology, philosophy holds itself free to criticize; they are for it problems. The teleological arguments of the older theologians have had to be left behind. "We are fearfully and wonderfully made," no doubt, but not perfectly, and the arguments in favour of an intelligent contriver (cf. The Bridgewater Treatises) which showed the greatest plausibility, were made meaningless by Darwin's work. Further, Evoluton knows no break. We cannot believe in the doctrines of the "fall" or in "original sin," for Evolution means a progress from lower to higher forms. Thus we see that many of the older forms of theological statement call for revision. Bergson has done much to stimulate a keener and fresher theological spirit which will express God in a less static and less isolated form, so that we shall not have the question asked, either by children or older folks, "What does God do?"

It should be noted before closing this section that the religious consciousness is tempted to take Bergson's views on Soul and Body to imply more than they really do. The belief in Immortality which Western religion upholds is not a mere swooning into the being of God, but a perfect realization of our own personalities. It is only this that is an immortality worthy of the name. To regard souls as Bergson does, as merely "rivulets" into which the great stream of Life has divided, does not do sufficient justice to human individuality. A "Nirvana," after death, is not immortality in the sense of personal survival and in the sense demanded by the religious consciousness.

The influence of Bergson's thought upon religion and theology may be put finally as follows: We must reject the notion of a God for whom all is already made, to whom all is given, and uphold the conception of a God who acts freely in an open universe. The acceptance of Bergson's philosophy involves the recognition of a God who is the enduring creative impulse of all Life, more akin perhaps to a Mother-Deity than a Father-Deity. This divine vital impetus manifests itself in continual new creation. We are each part of this great Divine Life, and are both the products and the instruments of its activity. We may thus come to view the Divine Life as self-given to humanity, emptying itself into mankind as a veritable incarnation, not, however, restricted to one time and place, but manifest throughout the whole progress of humanity. Our conception will be that of a Deity, not external and far-off, but one whose own future is bound up in humanity, rejoicing in its joy, but suffering, by a kind of perpetual crucifixion, through man's errors and his failures to be loyal to the higher things of the spirit.

Thus we shall see that, in a sense, men's noble actions promote God's fuller being. A Norwegian novelist has recently emphasized this point by his story of the man who went out and sowed corn in his late enemy's field THAT GOD MIGHT EXIST! [Footnote: The Great Hunger, by Johan Bojer.] But it is important to remember that in so far as we allow ourselves to become victims of habit, living only a materialistic and static type of existence, we retard the divine operations. On the other hand, in so far as our spirit finds joy in creative activity and in the furtherance of spiritual values, to this extent we may be regarded as fellow-labourers together with God. We cannot, by intellectual searching find out God, yet we may realize and express quite consistently with Bergson's philosophy the truth that "in Him we live, and move, and have our being."

CHAPTER XII
REFLECTIONS

Bergson not systematic — His style — Difficult to classify — Empirical and spiritual — Value of his ideas on Change, the nature of Mind, of Freedom — Difficulties in his evolutionary theory — Ethical lack — Need for supplement- Emphasis on Will, Creativeness, Human Progress and Possibilities.

In concluding this study of Bergson's philosophy, it remains to sum up and to review its general merits and deficiencies. We must remember, in fairness to Bergson, that he does not profess to offer us A SYSTEM of philosophy. In fact, if he were to do so, he would involve himself in a grave inconsistency, for his thought is not of the systematic type. He is opposed to the work of those individual thinkers who have offered "systems" to the world, rounded and professedly complete constructions, labelled, one might almost say, "the last word in Philosophy." Bergson does not claim that his thought is final. His ideal, of which he speaks in his lectures on La Perception du Changement — that excellent summary of his thought — is a progressive philosophy to which each thinker shall contribute. If we feel disappointed that Bergson has not gone further or done more by attempting a solution of some of the fundamental problems of our human experience, upon which he has not touched, then we must recollect his own view of the philosophy he is seeking to expound. All thinking minds must contribute their quota. A philosophy such as he wishes to promote by establishing a method by his own works will not be made in a day. "Unlike the philosophical systems properly so called, each of which was the individual work of a man of genius, and sprang up as a whole to be taken or left, it will only be built up by the collective and progressive effort of many thinkers, of many observers also, completing, correcting, and improving one another." [Footnote: Introduction to Creative Evolution, p. xiv. (Fr. p. vii).] Both science and the older kind of metaphysics have kept aloof from the vital problems of our lives. In one of his curious but brilliant metaphors Bergson likens Life to a river over which the scientists have constructed an elaborate bridge, while the laborious metaphysicians have toiled to build a tunnel underneath. Neither group of workers has attempted to plunge into the flowing tide itself. In the most brilliant of his short papers: L'Intuition philosophique, he makes an energetic appeal that philosophy should approach more closely to practical life. His thought aims at setting forth, not any system of knowledge, but rather a method of philosophizing; in a phrase, this method amounts to the assertion that Life is more than Logic, or, as Byron put it, "The tree of Knowledge is not the tree of Life."

It is because Bergson has much to say that is novel and opposed to older conceptions that a certain lack of proportion occasionally mars his thought; for he—naturally enough—frequently lays little emphasis on important points which he considers are sufficiently familiar, in order to give prominent place and emphasis to some more novel point. Herein lies, it would now appear, the explanation of the seeming disharmony between Intuition and Intellect which was gravely distressing to many in his earlier writing on the subject. Later works, however, make a point of restoring this harmony, but, as William James has remarked: "We are so subject to the philosophical tradition which treats logos, or discursive thought generally, as the sole avenue to truth, that to fall back on raw, unverbalized life, as more of a revealer, and to think of concepts as the merely practical things which Bergson calls them, comes very hard. It is putting off our proud maturity of mind and becoming again as foolish little children in the eyes of reason. But, difficult as such a revolution is, there is no other way, I believe, to the possession of reality." [Footnote: Lecture on Bergson and his anti-intellectualism, in A Pluralistic Universe. It may be remarked here that, although James hailed Bergson as an ally, Bergson cannot be classed as a pragmatist. His great assertion is that just because intellect is pragmatic it does not help us to get a vision of reality. Cf. the interesting work on William James and Henri Bergson, by W. H. Kallen.]

Bergson's style of writing merits high praise. He is no "dry" philosopher; he is highly imaginative and picturesque; many of his passages might be styled, like those of Macaulay, "purple," for at times he rises to a high pitch of feeling and oratory. Yet this has been urged against him by some critics. The ironic remark has been repeated, in regard to Bergson, which was originally made of William James, by Dr. Schiller, that his work was "so lacking in the familiar philosophic catch-words, that it may be doubted whether any professor has quite understood it." There is in his works a beauty of style and a comparative absence of technical terms which have contributed much to his popularity. The criticism directed against his poetic style, accuses him of hypnotizing us by his fine language, of employing metaphors where we expect facts, and of substituting illustrations for proof. Sir Ray Lankester says: "He has exceeded the limits of fantastic speculation which it is customary to tolerate on the stage of metaphysics, and has carried his methods into the arena of sober science." [Footnote: In the preface to Elliot's volume, Modern Science and the Illusions of Bergson, p. xvii.] Another critic remarks that "as far as Creative Evolution is concerned, his writing is neither philosophy nor science." [Footnote: McCabe: Principles of Evolution, p. 254.] Certainly his language is charming; it called forth from William James the remark that it resembled fine silk underwear, clinging to the shape of the body, so well did it fit his thought. But it does not seem a fair criticism to allege that he substitutes metaphor for proof, for we find, on examination of his numerous and striking metaphors, that they are employed in order to give relief from continuous abstract statements. He does not submit analogies as proof, but in illustration of his points. For example, when he likens the elan vital to a stream, he does not suggest that because the stream manifests certain characteristics, therefore the life force does so too. Certainly that would be a highly illegitimate proceeding. But he simply puts forward this to help us to grasp by our imaginative faculty what he is striving to make clear. Some critics are apt to forget the tense striving which must be involved in any highly philosophical mind dealing with deep problems, to achieve expression, to obtain a suitable vehicle for the thought — what wrestling of soul may be involved in attempting to make intuitions communicable. Metaphor is undoubtedly a help and those of Bergson are always striking and unconventional. Had Kant, in his Critique of Pure Reason, given more illustrations, many of his readers would have been more enlightened.

Bergson's thought, although in many respects it is strikingly original and novel, is, nevertheless, the continuation, if not the culmination, of a movement in French philosophy which we can trace back through Boutroux, Guyau, Lachelier and Ravaisson to Maine de Biran, who died in 1824. Qui sait, wrote this last thinker, [Footnote: In his Pensees, p. 213.] tout ce que peut la reflection concentree et s'il n'y a pas un nouveau monde interieur qui pourra etre decouvert un jour par quelque Colomb metaphysicien.

Many of the ideas contained in Bergson's work find parallels in the philosophy of Schopenhauer, as given in his work The World as Will and Idea (Die Welt als Wille und Vorstellung), particularly his Voluntarism and his Intuitionism. The German thinker regarded all great scientific discoveries as an immediate intuition, a flash of insight, not simply the result of a process of abstract reasoning. Schelling also maintained a doctrine of intuition as supra-rational.

Ravaisson, [Footnote: Ravaisson (1813-1900) wrote De l'habitude, 1832; La metaphysique d'Aristote, 1837; and his Rapport sur la philosophie en France au xix siecle, 1867. See Bergson's Memoir, 1904.] to whom Bergson is indebted for much inspiration, attended the lectures of Schelling at Munich in 1835. This French thinker, Ravaisson, has had an important influence on the general development of thought in France during the latter half of the last century, and much of his work foreshadows Bergson's thought. He upheld a spiritual activity, manifesting itself most clearly in love and art, while he allowed to matter, to mathematics and logic only an imperfect reality. He extolled synthetic views of reality rather than analytic ones. We are prevented, he said, from realizing our true selves because of our slavery to habit. To the ultimate reality, or God, we can attain because of our kinship with that reality, and by an effort of loving sympathy enter into union with it by an intuition which lies beyond and above the power of intellectual searching. As Maine de Biran foretold the coming of a metaphysical Columbus, so Ravaisson, in his famous Rapport sur la philosophic en France au xix siecle, published in 1867, prophesied as follows: "Many signs permit us to foresee in the near future a philosophical epoch of which the general character will be the predominance of what may be called spiritualistic realism or positivism, having as generating principle the consciousness which the mind has of itself of an existence recognized as being the source and support of every other existence, being none other than its action."

Lachelier, a disciple of Ravaisson, brought out—as has been already remarked [Footnote: Page 3.]—the significance of the operations of vital forces and of liberty. Guyau, whose brief life ended in 1888 and whose posthumous work La Genese de I'Idee de Temps was reviewed by Bergson two years after the publication of his own Time and Free Will, laid great stress on the intensification and expansion of life. Boutroux, in his work, has insisted upon the fact of contingency.

These forecasts of Bergson's thought made by men to whom he owes much and for whom he personally has the greatest admiration are interesting, but we are not yet able to look upon his work through the medium of historical perspective. We can however see it as the culmination of various tendencies in modern French philosophy; first, the effort to bring philosophy into the open air of human nature, into immediate contact with life and with problems vital to humanity; secondly, the upholding of contingency in all things, thus ensuring human freedom; thirdly, a disparagement of purely intellectual constructions as true interpretations of human life and all existence, coupled with an insistence on an insight that transcends logical formulation.

As a thinker, Bergson is very difficult to classify. "All classification of philosophies is effected, as a rule, either by their methods or by their results, 'empirical' and 'a priori' is a classification by methods; 'realist' and 'idealist' is a classification by results. An attempt to classify Bergson's philosophy, in either of these ways, is hardly likely to be successful, since it cuts across all the recognized divisions." [Footnote: Mr. Bertrand Russell's remark at the opening of his Lecture on The Philosophy of Bergson, before The Heretics, Trinity College, Cambridge, March 11, 1912.] We find that Bergson cannot be put in any of the old classes or schools, or identified with any of the innumerable isms. He brings together, without being eclectic, action and reflection, free will and determinism, motion and rest, intellect and intuition, subjectivity and externality, idealism and realism, in a most unconventional way. His whole philosophy is destructive of a large amount of the "vested interests" of philosophy. "We are watching the rise of a new agnosticism," remarked Dr. Bosanquet. A similar remark came from one of Bergson's own countrymen, Alfred Fouillee, who, in his work Le Mouvement idealist et la reaction contre la science positive, expressed the opinion that Bergson's philosophy could but issue in le scepticisme et le nihilisme (p. 206). Bergson runs counter to so many established views that his thought has raised very wide and animated discussions. The list of English and American articles in the Bibliography appended to the present work shows this at a glance. In his preface to the volume on Gabriel Tarde, his predecessor in the chair of Modern Philosophy at the College de France, written in 1909, we find Bergson remarking: On mesure la portee d'une doctrine philosophique a la variete des idees ou elle s'epanouit et a la symplicite du principe ou elle se ramasse. This remark may serve us as a criterion in surveying his own work. The preceding exposition of his thought is a sufficient indication of the wealth of ideas expressed. Bergson is most suggestive. Moreover, no philosopher has been so steeped in the knowledge of both Mind and Matter, no thinker has been at once so "empirical" and so "spiritual." His thought ranges from subtle psychological analyses and minute biological facts to the work of artists and poets, all-embracing in its attempt to portray Life and make manifest to us the reality of Time and of Change. His insistence on Change is directed to showing that it is the supreme reality, and on Time to demonstrating that it is the stuff of which things are made. He is right in attacking the false conception of Time, and putting before us la duree as more real; right, too, in attacking the notion of empty eternity. But although Change and Development may be the fundamental feature of reality, Bergson does not convincingly show that it is literally THE Reality, nor do we think that this can be shown. He does not admit that there is any THING that changes or endures; he is the modern Heraclitus; all teaching which savours of the Parmenidean "one" he opposes. Yet it would seem that these two old conceptions may be capable of a reconciliation and that if all reality is change, there is a complementary principle that Change implies something permanent.

Then, again, we feel Bergson is right in exposing the errors which the "idea of the line," the trespassing of space, causes; but he comes very near to denying, in his statements regarding duree pure, any knowledge of the past as past; he overlooks the decisive difference between the "no more" and the "not yet" feeling of the child's consciousness, which is the germ of our clear knowledge of the past as past, and distinct from the future.

To take another of his "pure" distinctions, we cannot see any necessity for his formulation of what he terms "Pure Perception." Not only does it obscure the relation of Sensation to Perception, but it seems to be quite unknown and unknowable and unnecessary as an hypothesis. As to his "Pure" Memory, there is more to be said. It stands on a different plane and seems to be the statement of a very profound truth which sheds light on many difficult problems attaching to personality and consciousness, for it is the conservation of memories which is the central point in individuality. His distinction between the habit of repeating and the "pure" memory is a very good and very necessary one. In his study of the relation of Soul and Body, we find some of his most meritorious work—his insistence on the uniqueness of Mind and the futility of attempts to reduce it to material terms. His treatment of this question is parallel to that of William James in the first part of his Ingersoll Lecture at Harvard in 1898, when he called attention to "permissive" or "transmissive" function of the brain. Bergson's criticisms of Parallelism are very valuable.

No less so are his refutations of both physical and psychological Determinism. Men were growing impatient of a science claiming so much and yet admittedly unable to explain the really vital factors of existence, of which the free action of men is one of the most important. The value placed on human freedom, on the creative power of human beings to mould the future, links Bergson again with James, and it is this humanism which is the supremely valuable factor in the philosophies of both thinkers. This has been pointed out in the consideration of the ethical and political implications of Bergson's Philosophy. Nevertheless, although his insistence on Freedom and Creative Evolution implies that we are to realize that by our choices and our free acts we may make or mar the issue, and that through us and by us that issue may be turned to good, the good of ourselves and of our fellows, there is an ethical lack in Bergson's philosophy which is disappointing. Then, as has been remarked in the chapter on Religion, there is the lack of teleology in his conception of the Universe; his denial of ANY purpose hardly seems to be in harmony with his use of the phrase "the meaning of life."

Much in Bergson would point to the need for the addition of a philosophy of Values. This, however, he does not give us. He shirks the deeper problems of the moral and spiritual life of man. He undervalues, indeed ignores, the influence of transcendent ideas or ideals on the life-history of mankind. The study of these might have led him to admit a teleology of some kind; for "in the thinking consciousness the order of growth is largely determined by choice; and choice is guided by valuation. We are, in general, only partially aware of the ends that we pursue. But we are more and more seeking to attain what is good, true and beautiful, and the order of human life becomes more and more guided by the consciousness of these ends." [Footnote: Professor Mackenzie: Elements of Constructive Philosophy, p. 111.] Bergson, however, will not ultimately be able to evade the work of attempting some reconciliation of moral ideas and ideals with their crude and animal origins and environment, to which they are so opposed and to which they are actually offering a very strong opposition. That he himself has seen this is proved by the attention he is now giving to the problems of social Ethics.

There are four problems which confront every evolutionary theory. These concern the origin of: Matter, Life, Consciousness, and Conscience. Bergson finds it very difficult to account for the origin of Matter, and it is not clear from what he says why the original consciousness should have made Matter and then be obliged to fight against it in order to be free. Then, in speaking of the law of Thermodynamics, he says: "Any material system which should store energy by arresting its degradation to some lower level, and produce effects by its sudden liberation, would exhibit something in the nature of Life." This, however, is not very precise, for this would hold true of thunder-clouds and of many machines. In regard to Instinct, it has been pointed out by several experts that Instinct is not so infallible as Bergson makes out. Of the mistakes of Instinct he says little. Dr. McDougall in his great work Body and Mind says, when speaking of Bergson's doctrine of Evolution: "Its recognition of the continuity of all Life is the great merit of Professor Bergson's theory of Creative Evolution; its failure to give any intelligible account of individuality is its greatest defect. I venture to think," he continues, "that the most urgent problem confronting the philosophic biologist is the construction of a theory of life which will harmonize the facts of individuality with the appearance of the continuity of all life, with the theory of progressive evolution, and with the facts of heredity and biparental reproduction." [Footnote: McDougall, Body and Mind, Footnote to p. 377.]

In the light of such criticism it is important to note that Bergson is now giving attention to the problem of personality which he made the subject of his Gifford Lectures. It is a highly important problem for humanity, and concentration on it seems the demand of the times upon those who feel the urgent need of reflection and who have the ability to philosophize. Can philosophy offer any adequate explanation of human personality, its place and purpose in the cosmos? Why should individual systems of energy, little worlds within the world, appear inside the unity of the whole, depending on their environment, physical and mental, for much, but yet capable of freedom and unforeseen actions, and of creative and progressive development? Further, why should ideals concentrate themselves as it were round such unique centres of indeterminateness as these are? On these problems of our origin and destiny, in short, on an investigation of human personality, thinkers must concentrate. Humanity will not be satisfied with systems which leave no room for the human soul. Human personality and its experience must have ample place and recognition in any philosophy put forward in these days.

Bergson's work is a magnificent attempt to show us how, in the words of George Meredith: "Men have come out of brutishness." His theory of evolution is separated from Naturalism by his insistence on human freedom and on the supra-consciousness which is the origin of things; on the other hand, he is separated from the Idealists by his insistence upon the reality of la duree. He contrasts profoundly with Absolute Idealism. While in Hegel, Mind is the only truth of Nature, in Bergson, Life is the only truth of Matter, or we may express it—whereas for Hegel the truth of Reality is its ideality, for Bergson the truth of Reality is its vitality.

The need for philosophical thought, as Bergson himself points out, [Footnote: See the closing remarks in his little work on French philosophy, La Philosophie.] is world-wide. Philosophy aims at bringing all discussion, even that of business affairs, on to the plane of ideas and principles. By looking at things from a truly "general" standpoint we are frequently helped to approach them in a really "generous" frame of mind, for there is an intimate connexion between the large mind and the large heart.

Bergson has rendered valuable service in calling attention to the need for man to examine carefully his own inner nature, and the deepest worth and significance of his own experiences. For the practical purposes of life, man is obliged to deal with objects in space, and to learn their relations to one another. But this does not exhaust the possibilities of his nature. He has himself the reality of his own self-consciousness, his own spiritual existence to consider. Consequently, he can never rest satisfied with any purely naturalistic interpretation of himself. The step of realizing the importance of mental constructions to interpret the impressions of the external world, and the applying them to practical needs, was a great advance. Much greater progress, however, is there in man's realization of qualities within himself which transcend the ordinary dead level of experience, the recognition of the spiritual value of his own nature, of himself as a personality, capable even amid the fluctuations of the world about him, and the illusions of sense impressions, of obtaining a foretaste of eternity by a life that has the infinite and the eternal as its inheritance; "He hath set eternity in the heart of man." Man craves other values in life than the purely scientific. "There are more things in heaven and earth than are dreamt of" in the philosophies of the materialist or the naturalist. Bergson assures us that the future belongs to a philosophy which will take into account THE WHOLE of what is given. Transcending Body and Intellect is the life of the Spirit, with needs beyond either bodily satisfaction or intellectual needs craving its development, satisfaction and fuller realization. The man who seeks merely bodily satisfaction lives the life of the animal; even the man who poses as an intellectual finds himself entangled ultimately in relativity, missing the uniqueness of all things — his own life included. An intuitive philosophy introduces us to the spiritual life and makes us conscious, individually and collectively, of our capacities for development. Humanity may say: "It doth not yet appear what we shall be," for man has yet "something to cast off and something to become."